A CANISTER OF
KNOWLEDGE

CAREER GUIDANCE AND PERSONALITY DEVELOPMENT

NORIEL E. BAÑES

PARTRIDGE

Copyright © 2019 by Noriel E. Bañes.

ISBN: Softcover   978-1-5437-4943-4
           eBook   978-1-5437-4944-1

All rights reserved. No part of this book may be used or reproduced by any means, graphic, electronic, or mechanical, including photocopying, recording, taping or by any information storage retrieval system without the written permission of the author except in the case of brief quotations embodied in critical articles and reviews.

Because of the dynamic nature of the Internet, any web addresses or links contained in this book may have changed since publication and may no longer be valid. The views expressed in this work are solely those of the author and do not necessarily reflect the views of the publisher, and the publisher hereby disclaims any responsibility for them.

Print information available on the last page.

To order additional copies of this book, contact
Toll Free 800 101 2657 (Singapore)
Toll Free 1 800 81 7340 (Malaysia)
orders.singapore@partridgepublishing.com

www.partridgepublishing.com/singapore

CONTENTS

Acknowledgment 1

Chapter 1: Preparations 2

    What your Curriculum Vitae looks like and how the recruiter sees and "seize" it 5

    How to Write a Cover Letter that Catches the Eyes of Hiring Personnel? 9

    These are What the Recruiters Need from You 11

    Tips Before Interview 13

    Top Questions asked During the Interview and the Reasons why they are Being Asked 15

    Suggested Tips on how to Secure a Job 18

    Must-Haves and To-Do Things in Looking for a Job......20

    7 Gestures that Kill your Chances of Getting the Job.....22

    Being Inquisitive: A Point of Favor Towards Employment 25

    How to Groom Yourself for Interview 28

    It is not WHAT you know, it is WHOM you know 30

    Leveraging Social Media to its Prime 32

How Confidence Affects Employer's Decision............34

The English Language: Its Effects and Values in
Recruiting..37

6 Reasons why Employees stay in their Jobs...............39

Ethics Towards Job Opportunities...............................42

Chapter 2: Thrive 46

Chocolates or Candies?..49

Best Things to do in Spending Your Vacation Leave......51

Bullying in the Workplace: An issue that should
never be ignored...54

Camaraderie in the Workplace....................................56

The effects of Slang in Corporate Communication.........59

Career Transition: Best ways to handle it....................60

How to Cope with Changes in the Organization.......63

How to handle Rejection on the Promotion
that was not Granted?..65

How to React and what to do on a Termination
Notice..67

Things to Remember before Resigning.......................69

Reasons why People keep Jumping
from one Job to Another..71

Why Employee Empowerment Vital for
Organizational Success?..74

Chapter 3: Creating a Better Version of Ourselves 78
How to Leave Good Impression that Lasts 81
Stress Management: Combating stress towards achieving targets 83
How to Maintain Productivity at Work 85
Suggestions on How to Expand your Vocabulary 87
5 Important Things that a Great Public Speaker Should Possess 90
6 Tips to Consider in Speaking before the Crowd 92
6 Essential Phrases and Sentences used by Great Leaders 95
Reading: A Habit worth the Expense of Time 97
11 Tips for Writing a Professional Email 99
8 Suggestions for Effective Study Habits 103
6 Important Definitions of Excellent Customer Service 107
How to be an Exceptional Telephone Conversationalist? 110
Simple Tips on How to Survive in College 112
These are 5 Things that make you a Professional 114
Tips for Writing a Stirring Graduation Speech 116

References 119

ACKNOWLEDGMENT

To the Lord God our Savior Who made all things possible, all the praises to You. To my best friend and brother, Mr. Darcy Mirasol, who helped the aesthetics aspect of the book and for pushing me to follow my dreams, thank you very much. And of course, to my parents who are my inspiration to be at my best all the time and to do more, my endless gratitude to you both.

Chapter 1

PREPARATIONS

This chapter will give us concepts and ideas in preparation for employment. It speaks loudly on establishing a kind of professional you should be while getting ready to be part of the employed professionals. Articles will be all about essentials in preparation for a successful job hunt. The chapter offers diversified tips and to do things from CV writing, creating an impressive cover letter, preparing for interview, up to building social networks that can help you gain referrals in landing a job.

"Arming ourselves with necessary *preparations* is perfecting what we love doing."

What your Curriculum Vitae looks like and how the recruiter sees and "seize" it

10 TIPS TO TOP UP YOUR CV

A top-of-the-art company recruitment officer's view on curriculum vitae

It's only a matter of 6 seconds for you to win the eyes and attention of the recruiter. According to Business Insider, recruiters spend an average of six seconds reviewing resumes before they could be able to make an initial decision whether to shortlist you or not. Having said that, you should strengthen your profile and must never leave a room for mistakes.

Writing your CV is a vital part of your success in the world of employment. It is a story of your life and it is up for you on how you create and design your story to catch your reader's attention. When you are given a whole lot of a virtual world, how are you going to design your world? How are you going to beautify it? Same goes with writing your CV. You must make it best but this time, back it up with the facts about yourself and experience. What does a good CV look like? I have done a little research about the simple complex of the CV and how it should look like.

1. **Be concise.** Writing is perhaps one of the most difficult tasks to some. But take into consideration that when writing, information should be correct and complete in only a matter of few words. Avoid long sentences and beat around the bush. Moreover, avoid words which do not give much impact to your skills and profile. Bear in mind that this is not a battle of how many high-sounding words or how figuratively beautiful you write, it is a matter of doing it right with the touch of simplicity and

straightforwardness. The University of Kent researchers said that the longer and denser your CV is, the harder it is for the employer or recruiters to comprehend your details. Do not put too many information. Only those that are important. After all, you leave a whole lot of something left for the employer during interview.

2. **Avoid Jargons.** It is better to state the information in a plain and simple English simply because it is easy to understand. It is fine to have some little technical terminologies included but it should match with kind of industry and position that you are applying for.

3. **Don't include Objectives.** It may sound silly but that should be it. When you apply for a job, it is understood that you want to be hired and that you wanted to work in an organization. This section is not necessary. Instead, write an executive summary. It is a part where you pitch in your strengths and interests, the kind of job that you are interested in, and a one sentence idea of your experience. Business Insider calls it a "30-second elevator pitch." It is like you put your best foot forward.

4. **Do not use pronoun I.** In writing, pronoun gives much impact to the quality and imagery of our short story. However, in writing CV, avoid using the first-person point of view because it is understood that everything in your CV is all about you and no one else.

5. **Use of Photo.** This is something that you have to think twice. In my opinion, it is not necessary to put your 2x2 picture in your resume unless you are applying to be an actor or a model. However, there are some companies which would require you to attach a photo then you may do so. British CVs don't usually put photograph.

Same goes with the USA. They believe that this may cause partiality for the equal opportunity rights and a photograph make it easier to reject a candidate because of ethnicity, gender, or age *(Business Insider).* If you want to include your photograph, please avoid photos that you normally upload on Facebook with a peace hand gesture. Use a professional photo with a formal attire, head and shoulder shot and smile.

6. **Use one format.** There are numerous templates and formats to use in building CVs online or using MS Office. However, be careful of using templates. Make sure that you use the appropriate ones and that it should look professional. Speaking of format, be mindful about the spacing and the font style you use in writing. Use one font style all throughout the pages. According to *Daniel Scocco* of the Daily Writing Tips, there is no need for you to use fancy details and designs such as colored background, fancy fonts and images, etc. these do not give importance to the information you are presenting.

7. **Work Experience comes first.** Your name is on the top part of the page and your contact details and perhaps professional links, followed by your executive summary. One of the most of important parts of your CV is your Work Experience. Arrange your experience from the recent to the oldest. However, if you are a well-experienced employee, do not include your half-century-ago experience. It does not give much importance for an experienced employee, instead summarize it and give a short overview.

8. **Educational Background is written at the bottom** unless you are a fresh graduate and that, it is very important for the employer to know your degree prior to

shortlisting you. Work experience should be highlighted and that is the common trend in hiring employees with experience.

9. **Be truthful.** No matter how good you feel about yourself but everything you have written in your resume are lies, there's a great chance for you to be caught red handed. Not to mention the fact that it is unethical. Do not put skills that you are not good at or you have zero knowledge about unless you want to look stupid when the recruiter asks you try or explain it further. Remember, facts and facts alone.

10. **Have a final touch.** This means, take good care of the English aspects of your resume. Double or triple check the grammar, spelling, and punctuations. Though there are some electronic devices and programs to use in detecting mistakes, they are not hundred percent accurate. It is advisable to read it many times or ask someone to read and edit it for you because you don't want to give the employer a bad impression about you.

All these information and details should be written well because it is vital in getting yourself hired. As I always say, the talent market is very competitive nowadays and you may want to consider them if you want to stay ahead of the competition. Writing a perfect CV may not still be enough to land you a job of your dream. You should also think of other aspects in hiring and sending in your application letter. Let us have a look at how you should write a comprehensive application letter that works best.

How to Write a Cover Letter that Catches the Eyes of Hiring Personnel?

ELEMENTS IN WRITING THE COVER LETTER THAT WORKS

A cover letter is the first thing that recruiters see in your job application. Might as well that it must be impeccable, and it should contain elements as that of the elevator pitch. One should build a strong and clear cover letter to sell the skills and potentials.

As I read through the websites while doing some simple research, I noticed that most of the points are different in ways that are dependent on the intentions of the applicants. However, I've come up with the general tips based on the common grounds. Below are tips for making it more convincing:

1. **Strong Opening.** According to the *monstergulf.com*, one should address the cover letter to the proper person. Make it personal and it should have a conversational tone and not arrogance. Start with something catchy and something strong like *"I am Project Management professional with 8-year intensive experience in Construction and oil and gas industry"*. Be direct to the point and your intention should be clear.

2. **Skills.** Highlight your skills and qualifications. Sell yourself and qualities that would make you a perfect fit for the job. Don't overdo it by listing down everything. Just write those that made you a superstar. With this, you may mention your previous achievements and contributions to your previous company.

3. **Short and Simple.** Do not compact all your achievements in one paper. Leave something for the interview. It is the key to have your application be read and shortlisted because nobody wanted to read a long cover letter with a bunch of idiomatic expressions and figurative languages.

4. **Close with a bang.** It is a distinct way of closing your letter with something that makes the reader want to meet you. According to *Glassdoor*, closing is the most important element that will help you land your next job interview. Integrate with confidence, enthusiasm, and call for action will make a big difference to your first step. You may write: *"I am eager to meeting with you to discuss further this fantastic opportunity, I will call you next week for the follow-up on my application and arrange for an interview."*

There are hundreds of ways to make a cover letter that works for you. But remember to always choose the best one because it is a vital stage in making your first step in your career a success. Many people ignore to write a cover letter upon sending their application, but it is one way for the employers to know the diligence and professionalism of the applicants. There are a lot of considerations to take but once perfected, it will come in handy to the job seekers and it will help a lot on their career search – speaking of professionalism and excellence.

These are What the Recruiters Need from You

QUALITIES AND TRAITS A CANDIDATE SHOULD POSSESS BEFORE AND AFTER THE INTERVIEW

Recruiters have spoken! There are many things in the checklist to tick in filling-up a position available in the organization. This checklist does not only contain skills and certifications needed for the job, but it contains the checklist of the "attitude" needed from an applicant. Sometimes, this part of the checklist appears in the recruiters' mind who's trying to observe your attitude and behavior during the interview.

I have done a simple research by communicating with the high caliber recruitment officers and Human Resource professionals on what they can say on the things needed from the applicants to land a job. Now, this information does not limit the skills and qualifications of the candidates, but this aims to provide ideas on the behavioral aspects of a person.

- **Positive body language**
- **Punctuality**
- **Tone of voice**
- **Confidence**
- **Honesty**
- **Team player**
- **Commitment**

Zenaida Requizo, *Human Resource Manager,* said that positive body language, punctuality, and the tone of voice comprised of attitude necessary from a candidate in order to be considered as a strong candidate. She also mentioned that confidence plays a big role in the interview. *"The candidate should be confident in what he or she is saying during the interview and that he must build a first good impression. Technical skills wise, knowledge of* *technology also helps since almost all processes are in digital, online, and computer-aided process".*

There are too many qualities a person possesses but honesty is what we always aim for. According to ***April Sampang,** Recruitment Consultant,* honesty is very important, not to mention someone who is a team player and is committed are by far the most important. True enough. Recruiters can engage you in the conversation to test your honesty and once lies are detected, it is a red flag.

As a recruitment Officer myself, I couldn't agree more on the above-mentioned list but let me just add a few more traits and qualities that a job-seeker must have. **Inquisitive** – For me, this is important and a good way to check whether a candidate is interested in the job or not. A candidate who raises sensible questions necessary to learn the ins and outs of the job is something. We do not assume that everyone understands the full job specifications in one sitting, but it is learned easily if you ask. It is true that sometimes we meet candidates who are not technically strong but if one shows interest, that is something to be considered. His enthusiasm to know, sparks interests and desire to be part of the organization.

These are just a few of the behaviors and attitudes to be considered and I am sure that a lot of HR practitioners could add more to this. We all want strong candidates who could make a difference in the company. It is just right that we need to look at these things because the success of a company is dependent on the qualities of the people working inside.

Tips Before Interview

5 TIPS TO POWER-UP YOUR JOB INTERVIEWS

Interviews is by far the most important part of the hiring process. It is one way for the recruiter to know whether all the information written on your profile are valid and accurate. Hence, it is, shall I say an investigation part where one is put into a friendly cross-examination to extract necessary information and at the same time, getting to know you more. Below are the tips before you get interviewed in the company:

1. **Be yourself.** It may sound cliché for some but is one way for you to introduce yourself as being the honest person you can be. There's no need for you to pretend to be another person that you're not-- especially if you are not a very good actor. Honesty is still the best thing you can give to the interviewer.

2. **Study well.** It is not like you're going back to high school or college and do the math or literature reviews, but it means a review of the job description for the position that you are applying. It is encouraged that one should practice before getting yourself in an interview. It would make you well-aware of the responsibilities that you are about to sign up for. This is also a way to be confident during the interview because it would help you convince the interviewer that you are knowledgeable on the subject. By studying well, it mean knowing the company's culture, their products and services, the kind of industry that they are involved in, and of course the people behind the success of the company.

3. **Dress-up.** We are being judged by the way we dress in an occasion or celebration. Same with interviews.

You will give a recruiter a whole bunch of ideas about your personality the way you present yourself. Your coat and tie or your business attire may not be as fancy as the attire of a CEO or top management people, but a perfectly professional look is more than enough to tell the recruiter that you can handle and organize yourself very well. This time, dress to impress but not to the point that it will make you feel uncomfortable with what you wear but a statement that you are smart and professional.

4. **Eye to eye Contact.** One of the most important things to bear in mind is the eye to eye contact with the interviewer. Never ever wander your eyes onto the ceiling or look down because the ceiling and the floor will never answer you back nor will ever give you credit. Looking at your interviewer straight to the eyes is an added value to your sincerity and interest to the job or topic being discussed. It is a non-verbal cue that means establishing a good connection or rapport to your audience.

5. **Magic word.** Please don't ever forget to show your gratitude to the interviewer or recruiter even if you don't get their assurance of passing you the interview or offering you the job. Saying "thank you "is one way to show respect, appreciation, and professionalism, not only to the recruiter but also to everyone you meet. Mind you, being polite and nice are hidden add-ons to you your credentials which will never be seen in one's resume.

Being authentic, prepared, professional, sincere, and polite are just some of the basic adjectives we should bear in mind in preparing for an interview. These will help us cater to the professional needs of the employers hence an additional flavor into the good culture that is being built by the leaders for a span of time. These behaviors tips are not just guidelines for a successful career journey, but also a professional development.

After knowing these tips before interview, it is a good time to prepare for the possible questions that may be asked during the interview. Let alone be the one who put bullets on the guns than the one who goes to a battle without them. The next topic will eventually help us at least gather some ideas on the possible questions and the rights ways to answer them on the interview potion of your job hunt.

Top Questions asked During the Interview and the Reasons why they are Being Asked

Finding a job is hard and so is the process. Organizations choose the best among the job seekers whom they can invest with for the benefit of the two parties. Therefore, competition is tough, and it is measured how well you do in the interview. Below are the top, perhaps the most common interview questions asked:

1. **Introduce yourself or tell me more about yourself.**

This aims to check how well you know yourself, strength, weakness, as well as your spontaneity. This does not expect you to answer what your name is, or anything stated in your CV, rather, your inner self which is not written in any documents.

How to answer this? You may start by what your close friends call you or what you are tagged as. Briefly explain the background of it and state how you do as an employee and your dreams and aspirations.

Sample: *My friends call me brainier instead of Raynier. It started when we were brainstorming for solutions and I was able to suggest an idea which they now consider as a great success in our work. I love being challenged and I'm hoping to sit one day with the big bosses thanking them for a promotion they'd offered me.*

2. **Why do you want to join our company?**

This aims to check how you see the company as a whole - their reputation, and their name over their competition, and how well you've done your research about the organization you are applying to. This measures how interested you are in the organization.

How to answer? Acknowledge the company status but don't overdo it. Go deeper by knowing what the company's mission and vision, and state what you share in common.

Sample: *I am impressed with how the company managed to stay humble despite the fame and awards received. But what really inspired me to join is the fact that this organization is driven by principles that promote employee's development and wellness. I believe that this company is my rightful place, and this company would find a perfect fit in me. This is an organization known to perform well. I wanted to make myself a part of an organization that does its best to provide clients' needs without compromising their employees' well-being.*

3. **Are you willing to extend beyond office hours?**

This aims to see what you can sacrifice for work, your commitment, and your dedication. Never lie. If you don't agree with the overtime, then say it with respect.

Sample: *I believe overtime is necessary when the task is not finished within an allotted time, which is why I manage my time very well to avoid an instance wherein we must prioritize work over our family.*

4. **How much is your asking salary?**

This checks whether their allotted salary would meet your demands. On the managerial side, this could also mean how confident you are with your skills. Be honest, at the same time be humble. After all, it is you who need them more than they would need you.

Sample: *I am hoping to see a figure higher than my previous pay, which is _____ for the reason that I also have spent much for my training and seminars, but I am open to negotiations regarding the figure.*

5. **Why did you leave your previous company?**

This checks for any issue you might be involved in, your work ethics, and how you respect your previous company. This also gives a notion that when you speak ill about your previous company, the tendency is you'll also speak ill of them when you leave. Remember that this prospect company can also contact your previous company and check how you were as an employee.

How to answer? State the reason for joining the prospect company rather than the reason you left your previous company. Never speak ill about your previous company.

Sample: *I am thankful for the skills I was able to develop in my previous position as a clerk. I believe it is about time to level up and I find this company the right venue to grow career wise -- a new environment… a new challenge, and a fresh perspective.*

These major ideas pointed out by *Mr. D. Mirasol* are the major points that HR professionals are taking into consideration. As an HR Professional, I backed it up with my experience in interviewing candidates for several positions, and mind you, it really does work in selecting the best candidate possible. A beautiful quote by *Kerry Stokes* probably summarizes all the major points and the reasons why employers wanted to select the best by interview. *"Ethics or simple honesty is the building blocks upon which our whole society is based, and business is a part of our society, and it's integral to the practice of being able to conduct business, that you have a set of honest standards."*

Suggested Tips on how to Secure a Job

4 IMPORTANT WAYS TO FIND A JOB HERE ABROAD

We may have different reasons why we seek employment. Others may say that they need a job to support their family. Others may reason out a professional fulfillment, and others may say to gain more money for the future. Whatever the reasons are, finding a job is not easy. Lucky for us, we were provided with diverse ways and tools to utilize in maximizing our job search. Below are the suggested tools to use:

1. **Make use of the free job portals online.** Jobs are present online in this world where technology is evolving. Gone are the antiquated techniques of posting jobs in the newspapers or in the flyers on the streets. There are many online job portals that you can utilize such as *bayt, indeed, naukrigulf, gulftalent, monstergulf,* to name a few. All you need to do is build a professional profile and explore job searches available in each of these portals.

Make sure to put an honest information and filter jobs that are relevant to your experience and industry.

2. **Use LinkedIn.** This is a very good tool in expanding your job search especially for a mid-level or higher position in the company. It provides you with the list of jobs available in the kind of industry that you have an experience with. Additionally, it will prompt you the list of vacancy that matches your job experience based on the profile that you created. This is also a great way of expanding your network of professionals to learn all about a certain company, updates or news about the industry, and more.

3. **Walk-in.** The line *"No pain, no gain"* does not only apply when you go to the gym, but it may be well fit when it comes to job hunting. We all know that applying for a job is exhausting especially when you're walking in. But it can elevate your chances of getting hired. The catch is, you do not just go out and submit yourself to the company's door randomly because there is always a big possibility that the companies you are going to may not be hiring and it is just a waste of your time and CVs. Always check online which companies are hiring and required candidates for a walk-in interview. That way, you are hundred percent sure that you are going to a company that accepts walk-ins. Again, always check the companies, get the address, and walk! Google is always your friend.

4. **Referrals or Network.** Be good with people around you because you won't know that they will be the one to introduce you to career opportunities. The friends of your friends should be your friends. Your network of friends can help a lot especially in finding a job. There

are companies that recommends referrals in filling-in the vacancies because it is a good way of creating harmony and good working environment. People who are comfortable with each other or who know each other well can create camaraderie and it is good for the company. Having said that, do not hesitate to ask your friends for a referral because you'll get a greater chance to land a job as someone being referred by an existing employee.

Your skills, attitude, and how well you do in the interview are still the important considerations in getting hired. Of course, these tips are just an aid for you to consider if you wanted to get a higher chance to land a job you desire. Trust yourself and embody positivity and that you'll get it. Be motivated by the reasons you needed the job. Nobody said it will be easy, but resilience and dedication are the keys to a successful job hunt.

Must-Haves and To-Do Things in Looking for a Job

We all know that finding a job is never easy and it takes a lot of effort in our part to at least get ourselves to be shortlisted and interviewed. One must arm himself with various things that would make him stand out among the rest. One should have an edge and the below are the suggested things one should possess in finding a job:

1. **Align your skills and background to the position you are applying for.** When applying for a job, it is important that you know your skills and capabilities and they should reflect on your CV. It should match the job requirement and it is easy for the recruiters or HR to place you in the right position. Knowing your skills and capabilities is as important as knowing the job itself.

So, do your homework, study the job description, and know a bit about it.

2. **Refine your CV or Resume.** Your *curriculum vitae* or CV reflects your personality and qualifications, so you better be sure of refining to make it look presentable. It must be short and full of action words that define your work history and the responsibilities done in your previous organization. Avoid grammatical errors and spelling mistakes because your CV is a professional document that sells you as a job seeker.

3. **Build Connection.** It is important to know people. They are the ones who could probably inspire you or push you to your limits and they are a great factor in successful career. Knowing professionals elevates your chances to getting a job you want. There are many ways to build connections: We socialize in some formal gatherings, we attend job fairs, build a pretty good profile on LinkedIn and add professionals in different fields, engage in social media, etc.

4. **Online Presence.** Speaking of social media, your online presence is as important as making connections. In today's digital world, one of the hiring strategies is employing the aid of technology and social media in search of great talents. People are active in social media, especially talented millennials. This is your next step towards getting employed.

5. **Job Portal Variations.** I am sure that we don't want to get stuck with just one easy way, we should utilize what is available for us. There are many job portals in which we could register our profile and apply such as monster, indeed, LinkedIn, bayt.com, naukrigulf, to name a few.

If you are not familiar with some of them, you have the internet to make it happen. I always recommend having various career portals to use in looking for a job because most of the companies are using some of them which are not necessarily the same as what the others are using. Be diverse and be smart!

6. **Technical Back-up or Certifications.** I strongly recommend investing in education and further studies to learn more skills. This is your arm on the battlefield and that would make you a strong candidate for the position. Many of you may say that learning new skills is a waste of time, but always remember that time is never wasted when you learn something new. It will enrich your professional knowledge and will advance you to the next step of your career.

Again, finding a job is never easy, I am sure many of you will agree but we must persevere. Perseverance should never be an option, it is a must. As what **Marie Curie** said, *"Life is not easy for many of us. But what of that? We must have perseverance and above all, confidence in ourselves. We must believe that we are gifted for something and that this thing must be attained."*

7 Gestures that Kill your Chances of Getting the Job

LIST OF THINGS YOU NEED TO STOP DOING DURING THE INTERVIEW

Our ways and gestures speak a lot about our personality and feelings. These non-verbal cues can be a candidate's downfall if not being considered carefully. There are those who do well in answering questions but are marked as lack of self-confidence because of their behaviors during the interview. It is vital for one to be aware of these non-verbal hints as they can be a make it or break it instance. Look at the below list of the things that you should avoid during the interview:

1. **Checking your watch.** I know that as a candidate, you may have a long list of interviews to attend to in a day or two but when you are right in the interview, it is not a good idea to keep on staring at your watch. It is an indication that you are in a hurry and that is not professional at all. It is an indirect way of saying that you have no time for the interview at all.

2. **Looking down or Looking up.** As an interviewer, I would probably say that a person who keeps on looking at the floor or looking up is a sign of disengagement and disinterest. Engage yourself in the conversation by looking the interviewer on the eyes. This is a strong signal that you are interested and that you are willing to learn and listen. Other than that, don't tell the interviewer that you are shy by looking down because you are there for him or her to know you better and what you can offer to the company.

3. **Biting your lips.** This gesture is subject to misinterpretation. Professionally speaking, someone who keeps on biting his lips may mean that he said something wrong. It may also mean dishonesty. Or nervousness. If your lips are dry, make sure to put a lip gloss or a lip balm prior to attending the interview to avoid this awkward gesture with the interviewer. Now let me tell you this, in an interview, biting your lips isn't sexy at all.

4. **Fillers.** Too many fillers during the interview may give a negative impact to the interviewer as it is an indicator of non-fluency in communication. I agree that this is most common to non-native English speakers but there are a lot of ways that we could minimize the fillers when we speak. Our "ahms" and "ahs" and even our excessive use of the word "like" in a sentence is a sign of non-fluency and it is cringeworthy. Many interviewers find the fillers cringy as they think that the candidates find it hard to express themselves in the interview.

5. **Fidgeting.** It is okay to be nervous sometimes because it may mean that you care. But do not make it obvious by fidgeting. There are people who do this especially when they feel nervous or over-excited. This is not a good sign for the employer when someone is fidgeting as it suggests a lack of preparation and you aren't ready for the interview. There are many suggestions on how to avoid nervousness in an occasion. Research on it and apply them before attending an interview.

6. **Over-nodding.** This is awkward and unpleasant to see. Over-nodding is perhaps the most annoying thing during the interview. When you agree, you can say a simple "yes" and a single nod. Do not over-do it because it is an exaggeration of agreement and it is not good. No matter how well you do credential wise but if you are annoying, it says so much about your personality and that other employees may not be well-pleased with you.

7. **Poor hygiene.** When you attend your interview, make sure that you are at your best not just mentally but hygienically as well. Have a proper haircut and well-combed hair, shave your mustache (for men). There are many interviewers who are allergic to strong perfume,

so it is a good idea to wear a mild-scented one. Wear an antiperspirant or a deodorant especially during the summer time. Make sure your socks don't smell, your clothes are ironed, and your shoes are polished. Doing otherwise may mean a lack of preparation and it tells so much about your poor time management.

Acting professionally will literally give you a positive feedback from the interviewer. You should be aware of your non-verbal behaviors as they most likely add to the negative impact on you. I am sure that the list goes on about the things you should avoid doing during the interview and I will just leave the rest for you. However, always remember that a strong candidate does not stop from being mentally ready but behaviorally as well. Again, these gestures speak something about your personality as an employee or as an individual.

These reminders are to watch out for because impression seems to get you a long way for a successful hire. This may sound simple but very intricate, and a salt to a blunt course. The next article will discuss about how one should respond and ask questions as a form of interest towards the opportunity.

Being Inquisitive: A Point of Favor Towards Employment

DOS AND DON'T'S OF ASKING QUESTIONS DURING INTERVIEW

It is human nature to ask if something is vague or needs further explanation. Same goes during interviews. It is expected for the candidate to ask as many questions as possible. Being inquisitive can be an additional point for a candidate towards landing a job. However, being inquisitive can also put you in deep waters and it may mean a red flag for the hiring personnel. Having said that, we should filter the questions we should ask during the interview. Below are the dos and don'ts in asking questions:

1. **Ask for a professional development plan.** It is just right to ask about the plans that the company has in store for you. It only shows that your intention in joining the company is not just about the salary, but a professional development that you can look forward to. There's no harm in asking because it is your right as a candidate to know your future in the company, especially in terms of professional growth.

2. **Don't ask questions that have been answered already.** Sometimes, when we force ourselves to think of questions for the sake of asking, we tend to ask a none sensible one. Tendencies are, we ask something that we already know the answer. Sometimes we repeatedly ask those that have already been discussed during the interview. Avoid it once and for all because you will sound ridiculous and you'll appear to be someone who has the lack of listening abilities.

3. **Ask for your goals and what is expected of you.** There are times when verifications are needed especially if the job description is a bit vague and you need clarifications. You may ask this kind of question for you to know well the things that you have to do in order to be successful in your position. The set goals and targets are best ways to motivate employees and will be a deciding factor for you whether to accept the job or not. Having a clear goal and the things that are expected of you to do can make your stay in a company a meaningful career journey.

4. **Don't ask how many candidates are being interviewed.** This is perhaps a big NO to ask an interviewer. Apparently, it is not your business whether the employer has dozens of interviews to conduct. You are there to do your best in the interview and to present yourself the best ways possible to make them like you. "Asking this kind of question will give the interviewer an impression that you are a little naïve and that it raises a question what your purpose of asking and it is quite awkward," Said **Alison Green.**

5. **Make follow-up questions if necessary.** To make things straight, it is just right to ask clarifications if necessary. It is a privilege that's given to the candidates as that will give you an opportunity to understand the information. It will also give the interviewer an idea that you are really interested in getting the job. Someone who does not give a damn about anything is an indication of being disinterested.

6. **Don't ask general questions.** This point will give you another idea that general questions limit the information that one can get from the interviewer. If you wanted to find out more details, be specific with your questions. It should not be a Yes or No question as it will not generate a good and clear result. Also, specific questions or open-ended questions create thorough discussions and it can build rapport between the candidate and the interviewer. If you want to be successful with your interview, make sure that you are conversant enough to throw questions that are worth discussing.

Many candidates should be aware that asking questions is crucial to landing a job. You can show your interest by asking sensible questions and that will be a point for your favor. I am sure that there will be thousands of questions in your mind, but you can filter them out by choosing the right ones. Make sure that you'll get the answer you're looking for because it will benefit you as someone who is seeking a better career.

"The Art and Science of asking questions is the source of all knowledge." – Thomas Berger

How to Groom Yourself for Interview

DRESS TO WEAR AND TRINKETS TO CONSIDER FOR INTERVIEW

It's only a matter of time when a recruiter will decide whether to hire you or not. Therefore, you must leave a good impression not only by your skills but also by how you dress up for interview. The Below list is the recommendations drawn from research by the experts.

1. **Wear a business attire**. Speaking of business attire, I mean a formal attire and that calls for a tie and suit. Long sleeves for men, with black or blue coat depending on your taste. Make sure to match the color of your tie to your inner shirt. If your inner is dark, your tie should be light in color and versa. For women, a black or blue blazer and a skirt or slack pants work. The rule is simple like that of the men. You don't need a fancy wear, but comfort and smart outfit count a lot.

2. **Belt and shoes**. A leather shoe, black or brown is congruent to formality. Note that the color of your belt should be the same as the color of your shoes. Always remember to shine your shoes so it will look nice and clean!

3. **Socks.** This is probably the least thing that will ever occur in your mind in preparing for your interview outfit. But these little garments really matter a lot when it comes to professionalism. Black socks really suit in whatever color of your suits, sleeves, or belt you have. It is a generic color that projects elegance. Make sure it doesn't smell because no matter how clear you look like, if your socks smell, then it is a disappointing impression.

4. **Watch and Jewelries.** Glittery jewelries and accessories should be left at home. You are not going to ball or a fashion show. A watch to wear doesn't have to be expensive and please leave your G-shocks or that of the sports watches you have because you are not running or climbing a mountain – it would be inappropriate. According to **Timothy Barber**, *Editor of watch World*, "Opt for a slimmer watch with your interview suit and try to find one you can wear with cufflinks so that it doesn't ruin the line of your sleeve."

5. **Hair and make-up.** Men are encouraged to cut hair an average length that matches your personality. A tidy-look haircut makes a great impression about yourself. Apply a hair gel or hair wax to make you look fresh. Women should wear a light make-up and please do not overdo it as you are not attending a beauty pageant or some sort.

It's not always the skills and credentials that matter, your appearance counts in landing a job. Your looks reflect your personality and professionalism. It is a measurement on how you take care of yourself and manage your time well. *America's Workplace Guru*, **Stephen Vicusi** says that the secret to landing a job is distinguishing yourself from the competition, that is, from the other people interviewing for the same job. It is a combination of each of these characteristics with intangibles, such as chemistry and those little personal things that separate you from everyone else.

A professional looking candidate has a high chance of getting hired as it exudes confidence and preparedness.

It is not WHAT you know, it is WHOM you know

THE POWER OF NETWORKING IN A JOB SEARCH

In the world of employment where competition is high, the demands for the right skills and experience are shooting up. Apart from the fact that degree and sets of training is important, there is another factor that is equally important – the people you know or your network. Some of you may find it odd knowing the there is a competition and sometimes you treat other people as competitors. But it is wrong. There might be competition in the world of employment but people around you are also the people who may be able to help you in your job search. Here are the top reasons why:

1. **Referrals.** *Human Resources Today* says that employee referrals are on the rise. Referred new hires are often a better fit when it comes to culture, they are more engaged, less likely to leave, and more productive. Do not underestimate the power of referrals because It is important for all the job seekers to know that companies want to bring in the right people into the organization. The more people you know, the more chances that you'll get to know companies and vacancies. You may expand your network in **LinkedIn, Facebook, twitter,** and other social media for that matter. We are in the age of digitalization, and these social media are exactly the

right platforms to use in expanding your network of professionals if you want to search for a job.

2. **Updates/News.** Apparently, your friends and acquaintances will bring you to their world, may it be through photography, beautiful sceneries that they've gone to, and other excursions they took. They are also the people who will give you news and updates about their organization should the company news page isn't enough to gather news from. They can give you honest feedback about their organization, the culture of their company, and the kind of environment they work with. This information will arm you, as a job seeker, to know more about the internal feels of the company. It will make you assess whether you are good at that kind of organization or not.

3. **Camaraderie** – One of the great pleasures in life is to work, and at the same time working with people that you are comfortable having around. Networking, building trust, and friendship can make a huge difference in creating a friendly environment. Should you leave the company, these people or your friends can write you a good recommendation for your next career journey. Note that most of the companies do background checks to know what kind of employee you have been and if you are someone who creates a good working environment among others.

Sadly, people are not fully aware of the implications and importance of networking. Nowadays, there is a negative connotation to the word as if that networking is filthy and unethical activity. But if you come to think of it, networking, on its other side, provides greater opportunities in your job search.

Leveraging Social Media to its Prime

THE INFLUENCE OF SOCIAL MEDIA TO EMPLOYMENT AND BRAND BUILDING

Just one click of a mouse and the news spreads like a ripple in the ocean. Social media is prevalent and indeed used as a platform to share updates, information, and one's thoughts. We cannot stop the power of social media in connecting with the world and its dominations. However, aside from the purpose that we already know such sharing feelings and photos, spreading gossips and heartaches, social media have something more to offer. Let us talk about its use for employment and brand building. Below are the things you can do with it:

1. **Platform for employment.** According to *Statista*, Facebook have had 1.86 billion active users in the fourth quarter of 2016 and it is considered the most popular social network worldwide. There are 310.1 Million users of twitter, and LinkedIn has over 467 million members worldwide. Having said that, how many do you think are logging in to check employment updates? Recruiters are now using social media to post vacancies and used it as a hiring platform. It is a very effective podium in recruiting and sourcing the right candidates to fill-in the job. LinkedIn, for example, is designed to do that. Most certainly, Facebook groups can be created to recruit and find talent, or you may want to follow a certain recruiter or recruitment agencies on twitter. Build your career using social media - it's just right there in front of you.

2. **Platform to develop business.** With the aid of technology and these social media platforms, building a company's identity and brand have become easier nowadays. **Chris Ferdinandi** has a great statement about this. *"Every time*

you talk about your organization's culture, you build your company brand." This will help people understand your core business, your values at work, and your mission and vision. Twitter and Facebook find their ways to have it known to the world. SEOs would explain it better as technology is so handy. Tweet your organization, talk about it, share it on Facebook, and create a brand in LinkedIn. That way, marketing is much more effective than the primitive ways such as fliers and radio broadcast because majority of us now is in the face of these giant network sites.

3. **Build connection with the professionals.** I think this is the best solution for those who wanted opportunities to knock on their doors. Again, don't just wait for the opportunity to knock, create them and do something! I believe you are a step closer to your dream job or business success if you know how to find them. Connecting with the professionals worldwide makes it easy for one to do it. Use them to contact the management, HR professionals, and people who are involved in the business. Updates are provided along with company's twitter account, so follow. Updates are made in Facebook account, so like, share and read. Updates are shared in LinkedIn so apply!

4. **Platform for research.** Research centers, if not all, are present in social media. Public and private organizations are there too! A lot of information is shared as public domain and some share for payment. Whatever you want it for, you can get updated information that you need which are drawn from research, tests, and surveys. Those businessmen, scholars, writers, publishers, and experts in social media make it easy for you to do your

primary and secondary research. Again, they can be your connections!

5. **Skills and professional development.** Certainly, you can acquire skills because some private organizations are giving a lot of training topics that are present in social media such as LinkedIn. There are a lot of free training that you can register on or if you wanted certifications, you may want to pay for it as well. The thing is, all these can now be done using this site. It is a perfect way of developing your talent and skills without compromising your time in going to the classroom and listening to the lectures. With these, you can learn at your most convenient time and at the comfort of your home.

There's no wrong with sharing photos and sharing love shout-outs and blahs in social media. We can use it for personal and professional gain instead because it is not only limited for a pleasure that it offers but to develop our lives. They are created for us to use and gain something from. Twit, share, like, shout-out, update, and post good and useful information for gains. So the question is, what is in your mind?

How Confidence Affects Employer's Decision

CONFIDENCE MAKES OTHER PEOPLE CHANGE MINDS

"To be yourself in a world that is constantly trying to make you something else is the greatest accomplishment." - Ralph Waldo Emerson

This line by Ralph Waldo Emerson gives us the ability to transform ourselves into someone that we're not used to be. It talks about confidence and the ability to accomplish so much in life. Confidence gives others the impression that anything is possible, and that strong presence is a huge factor in searching for employment. Below are the reasons why confidence is important in seeking for a job.

1. **Confidence is a skill.** This idea best represents confidence. It is a skill although it can't be mastered overnight but it can be learned and developed in due time. This is a plus point to your credentials in applying for a job. According to *Jim Taylor, Ph.D.*, confidence is the most important psychological contributor to performance in the business world because you may have all the ability in the world to accomplish a goal, but if you don't believe you have that ability, you won't use that ability to its fullest extent in pursuit of success.

2. **Confidence is the key to success and basis for high level of productivity.** I second this idea of *Chitra Reddy*. It is the basis of the ability to accomplish the obstacles and it goes down to our belief. We attain a certain degree of productivity if we believe in ourselves and that we are confident enough - confident to face people, face the challenge, and even face the problems. A person who does not have the confidence is a person who is afraid to win.

3. **Confidence is a series of ideas that speaks possibility.** Confidence is different from lie. You would surely know if the person is confident at what he says compare to the person who brags and lie all the time. Now, this is important in your job application if you want to win the decision of the employer and get the job. Exude

confidence and show them you can do the job and it is possible for you to get it. You are there because you believe in yourself and that you are armed with essential skills that can make you successful. Employers like confident people because again, it is good for business.

4. **Confidence is a key to a successful job search.** This is very true. Nothing will happen to a person who does not stand up for himself or someone who is too shy to face people. ***Staphanie Maxwell*** has some good idea and she said, *"If you have the slightest hesitation, do what it takes to change this mindset. As a confident person, you will present yourself in a markedly different way, leading to a much greater chance of getting the job you want."* Talent is very competitive nowadays and that people who have extraordinary skills and attitude can get through the world of success in the place of employment.

This one skill makes all the difference in your life as a job seeker or employee. If you want to be successful in your chosen endeavor, the very basic thing to do is to believe in yourself that you can be successful, that you can do it all, that you are not afraid to take the risk and face the challenge. After all, we are the one who creates our own future.

Something to ponder:

"Every day, I always tell myself: I am great! I can do it! And that I have what it takes to be successful."

The English Language: Its Effects and Values in Recruiting

THE TREND IN RECRUITING ENGLISH SPEAKING TALENTS

I was very surprised when I was flipping through websites looking for some good articles to read. I came across with the language proficiency article and employment opportunities. It is said that **65%** of recruiters and hiring managers say strong written or spoken communication skills are more important in an entry-level job applicant than their college major, and strong communicators have a competitive edge *(Gallo, C. -Forbes)*.

We are in the world where there is a shortage of talent and that is hard to find. Someone must have the right attributes for the growing industry and by that, I mean communication is a great factor. Someone who has good communication skills has an edge in the competition. Below are just some reasons why it is considered as a great factor in hiring:

1. **English becomes the widely used language in business.** Surely, hiring managers don't want to take risks on someone who has a poor sentence construction, or someone who cannot create a comprehensive sentence. Business is greatly affected by miscommunication and perhaps it means a loss of profits if we want to put it in a grave situation. The English language is hard to master considering its complexities and rich vocabularies. However; non-native speakers can learn the language through constant practice, training, and reading. There are short courses offered on basic, intermediate, and advanced English language learning. Why don't we enroll and start learning the language?

2. **Confidence.** Strange as it may sound, but someone who speaks English well is congruent to confidence. It may mean to some hiring managers or recruiters that you can talk to anyone. You can communicate your mind and express your thoughts effectively, and that is important to business. Hiring personnel would choose someone who speaks his mind effectively using the language that is used universally.

3. **Smart attribute.** Someone who communicates well in English appears as being "smart." In my experience as a hiring officer, we always go for someone who has a strong command of English language because technical skills can be learned, but soft skills such as English fluency is integral and that needs to be taken into major consideration. Speaking is an art that cannot be taught in one session or two. We all know that business could not function without communication from inside and outside the organization. It is smart when you have the power to influence the minds and decision of stakeholders and investors through effective and smart communication. In other words, we need smart people in our business.

4. **It is needed for customer service.** We build a business to attract customers and earn. To earn a lot, one should satisfy his customers in a way that both parties are not compromised. It is done through effective communication skills especially for international companies that are trying to expand and improve its presence globally. Comforting words, assurance, willingness to help and eagerness to build rapport to customers, are best expressed when you have a strong foundation of English language at your purse.

More companies are into globalization right now and that means attracting customers worldwide. It is done when you know how to speak to everyone and communicate in both written and spoken English. Giant countries such as the USA and Europe, China (starting to invest for English language Education) are some of the big countries that invest business globally and the English language is used. Great opportunities are open to those who speak, understand, and write better English.

6 Reasons why Employees stay in their Jobs

CHOOSING THE RIGHT EMPLOYER

Many of us have found ourselves on our desks in front of a computer. Some find themselves comfortable being in front of the students teaching. Some deal business with the customers, and some fix plates, tables, chairs, and cooks for our ladies and gentlemen. No matter what we do, we are in a job. But the question is, how do we get into that kind of job and what made us stay in the kind of environment we are in?

Our decisions affect our future and that is a great factor why we continue to live the kind of employment we have. Most of us are happy with it, some are aspiring for more, and some seemed to be contented. For us to grow professionally, we must take into consideration and decide intelligently, the kind of company that we should spend our time into. There are factors to consider and bear in mind the reasons why people stay or leave their company.

1. **Compensation.** Employees stay if they are properly compensated. That is one of the major reasons why people get into a job no matter what it takes. In fact, this

should not be in question at all because we work for us to be paid. We work for us to provide the needs of our family – food on the table, decent clothes, comfortable house, education for our children, vacation, etc. We must look for a company that provides well-compensated terms to its employees. Unfortunately, some companies do not consider their employees as customers. Employees are the internal customers and that we should take care of our internal customers first for it is very difficult to work, and at the same time be efficient with an empty stomach.

2. **Career Growth.** I am a firm believer of excellence and that it can be achieved if one finds himself growing and feels great at what he does. This is done if you are doing what is expected of you to do and even surpassing or exceeding your employer's expectations. Once you live up to the specific standards of the company, there will be a great chance for you to be advance your career. You just need to do a great job through experience and learn as much as you can. However, it is not as easy as one, two, and three. You need to be passionate. Now bear in mind the KPI (Key Performance Index) used as a tool in measuring how well you do in your designation. Employees love to stay in this kind of environment where efforts and service are recognized. Added to that, employees stay when there is a room for career and professional growth.

3. **Promotion.** Speaking of workplace recognition, promotion is a great factor why employees are loyal to their employer. It is one thing other than monetary aspect, that most of the workers or staff are after. It is one way for them to be motivated and do more as it always feels nice to know that your hard work and

perseverance paid off. In a workplace, there are lots of competitions and it's just right that those who are doing very well and are productive in their tasks deserve to be acknowledged by promoting them. Who wouldn't want to be promoted? After all, a promotion means a raise.

4. **Trust.** As they say, trust is earned, and it is something that is very difficult to give to someone. However; in the world of employment, it is a vital aspect that an employee needs in order to survive and do great in their job. Who would want a boss who sneaks around to his subordinates? Who would want a boss who puts CCTV Camera on each table of his colleagues? Who would want a boss who checks on you and your email every second and see if you're doing your job or not? Trust is important and that is an empowerment that means everything to the employees.

5. **Employee engagement.** There are no better ways in making our organization a better place to work with than having very engaging activities. An engagement does not only mean physical activities that make it lively, but also having our employees involved in decision making with the important tasks or decisions to make. Their ideas matter a lot and every single idea can make a difference. It makes our employees feel important and that their voices and opinions are heard and taken into consideration. It is difficult to leave an organization that promotes engagement to their employees and even those who left chose to go back.

6. **Learning and development.** To achieve greatness at work, one must be competitive enough to do his duties and responsibilities. That is why most of the companies put emphasis on the Learning and Development

programs for their employees. Millennial employees are very adaptable to changes and easily get bored especially if they don't find a challenge in their job anymore. Why not provide them programs for learning and develop their talents and skills? Hone their talents and use their skills to the optimum level. Some employees find it more challenging especially if they know something new. Most employees seek to learn, find their potentials, and love personal development. Mind you, most of the companies use training and development to retain talent.

These are just some of the reasons why employees stay in their organization. Perhaps they find it good for themselves and they are satisfied with what they have. If you are an individual seeking for career, or an employer trying to attract talents, you may want to regard the above points.

Ethics Towards Job Opportunities

THE WAY YOU SHOULD SEE THE EMPLOYMENT OPPORTUNITY

As basic guidelines and ethics in today's generation, it is imperative that one should be professional enough to deal with utmost civility. If you are looking for a job, there are certain behaviors that you should observe. These behaviors identify you as someone who is deserving of the job that you are applying for. Below are the tips and considerations to take:

1. **Always answer the phone call or emails sent by the recruiter or HR personnel.** There are times when you are caught up with a lot of stuff on your plate and that hinders you from responding to a very simple email

from a recruiter. However, always find time to at least have the courtesy to return the phone call or send out a response. You are the one who needs the job and the recruiters or HR people are giving you the opportunity to take a first step towards it. Have at least the decency to communicate.

2. **Be honest**. This simple reminder has been with us for ages. We even see this line posted in every classroom we attend to during our elementary days. Why is it so hard for some job seekers to follow even during the initial phone calls? Be truthful in everything that you say and do. Otherwise, dishonesty will put you in deep waters if you'll get caught red-handed. Be true to your words. When you said you could come for the interview on the specific date given, please come. If you can't make it, then inform the recruiter ahead of time. Recruiters have a boss and other decision maker to set up an appointment to interview you. Now if you make them wait and you cancel the last minute, you are wasting their time and you'll eventually build a bad reputation.

3. **Avoid tardiness and don't be lazy**. As famous as early bird catches the worm, tardiness is another behavior that a job-seeker should avoid. It is not a good idea to come to your appointment 30 minutes late. It says something about your terrible time management skills. Do not be lazy as it is not the word that a job-seeker should know. Wake up early and prepare your clothes for the interview the night before your appointment. That way, you don't have to cram as you have everything ready. Come at least 15 minutes early so you have enough time to feel the vibes of the company and the environment.

4. **Do not keep the employer hanging.** Keep your words as they say. Always have this *palabra de honor*. When you were already given an offer and you already accepted it and said yes, report to the company and update the concerned person about your whereabouts and status. Do not play games as it not in your vocabulary as a job-seeker to just quit in the middle of the recruiting process especially if you're already hired and the documents are ready for processing. Always remember that opportunity knocks only once. If you have doubts and disagreements, do not accept the job and tell the recruiters right away that you wanted to look for another opportunity.

5. **Be polite.** Politeness is equal to likable. This is one of the good traits that a job-seeker should possess. It means respect and decency. This characteristic has been the values we learn from our forefathers and it is right to take it to our professional lives. Ask and answer politely. Only then that we gain the respect of others. It does not hurt to be polite, use it to your advantage to make the recruiters or employers like you. In fact, it should come out naturally to all of us especially if you are looking for a job.

6. **You don't always get the help you deserve.** Sadly, not everyone can help you achieve your goal to land a job, not even the recruiters. They have certain guidelines to follow in order to be efficient in their job. They are not superman who will provide everything for you and will always give you the advantage compare to others. If you can't get the offer, please do not give up. Instead, learn from it and make it as a reason to improve yourself more. Arm yourself with knowledge, expand your network, and learn new skills to prepare you to your next job search.

It must be exhausting to look for a job especially if there is a competition for talents. Your skills and background count a lot but don't forget that your character and behaviors matter the most. As a recruiter, we need people who have the good attitude towards work. We don't need people who are skillful but is full of himself. We need people who are punctual, professional, and trainable. After all, skills can be developed but character and attitude cannot. This information on ethics for job seekers may sound so basic to some, but I feel that I have the need to write all these for people to enlighten some of us. We need to build our name in a good way. We need reminders even if it means that we go back to basic.

Chapter 2

THRIVE

As many strive for a successful career, there are also many things to bear in mind to make it happen. Things that need to acquire, practice, and develop such as the skills and right attitude in the office setting are what make the career a smooth sailing journey.

"The great flaw there is, is when you refuse to try and take a *risk*."

Chocolates or Candies?

REWARDS THAT WILL COME A LONG WAY IN MOTIVATING PEOPLE

"One might think that the money value of an invention constitutes its reward to the man who loves his work. But... I continue to find my greatest pleasure, and so my reward, in the work that precedes what the world calls success." - **Thomas Edison**

The psychology of reward system has been in the history of mankind for centuries. There are different forms of reward that one can offer. It can be a sack of salt, a bag of potatoes, or a sack of rice in exchange of the services. No matter what kind of reward one must receive, it surely reflects a job well done. In a corporate setting, the HR department will probably give out a trip for two to Paris, or an extended vacation once you hit your target or exceed expectations. It is just a matter of giving employees the right incentives that tickle their motivation to do better.

1. **It drives engagement.** Being employed is more than just receiving a salary and benefits. It is having a healthy working environment with the opportunity to grow and at the same time having fun. People still choose an environment with good employee engagement program glued with performance-based incentives. Rewards develop a team effort to achieve goals and will eventually create a fun-filled environment and a sense of belonging.

2. **Improves retention.** The cost of hiring can be very expensive. Therefore, a company should have a strong retention program. Rewards and incentives are one of the major factors that make employee stay in their

job. "When employees quit, it cost the business time and money, and may even disrupt the already effective workflow." – **Saint Mary's University of Minnesota.** According to the same article, base salary and benefit will only make employees work at the level that is required for them. A company should provide them with the opportunity to earn additional pay, perks, and recognition if they want employees to perform at a high level and stay in the organization for long.

3. **Motivates Employees and improves performance.** Performance-based appreciation or reward drives motivation among employees. Employees do feel good being appreciated on a job well done. As simples as posting an announcement in a bulletin board as Employee of the month can tickle motivation thus, it makes employees happy and acknowledged. According to *Ethan Pendleton*, the offer of an additional reward gives an employee an additional motivation to go above and beyond. By giving rewards, it is also essential to match what the employee need. Example, a family-man can be offered an additional vacation leaves to spend with his family, or a vacation with his kids for a day or two. Employees who can be considered as well-compensated may unlikely appreciate monetary incentives, but we should think of a non-monetary reward that would honor him.

As mentioned, the reward system or program can cost money. Perhaps it may even consume a chunk from the budget of HR that needs to be considered. However, there are also rewards that are non-monetary. As a company, we just need to be creative enough to think about the welfare of our employees. All individuals are unique and so people have different needs. Interests and wants may vary from person to person. To sum it up, rewards and incentives are necessary to drive engagement and create a fun and productive environment, it improves retention which makes employees find it hard to leave the company, and it motivates and improves employees' performance. All these can enhance over-all business performance. It may sound expensive as the Finance department may argue, but it delivers an effective return of investment. No matter how big or small, monetary or non-monetary, chocolates or candies, it still increases employees' motivation towards work do better and succeed.

Best Things to do in Spending Your Vacation Leave

SUGGESTED ACTIVITIES AND PLANS IN SPENDING THE ANNUAL LEAVE BENEFIT

A lot of times, we encounter professional burn-out. With all those inevitable long hours at work, we cannot help but feel exhausted and drained. That is why the government has mandated that all private and public companies must have annual leave for all their employees. The question is, how one should take advantage of this benefit from the company that is rightfully yours? Here are the top suggestions:

1. **Go home and visit your family.** "Home sweet home" as they say and "There's no place like home". This has been an old fashion that never gets old. For some people, they work abroad to provide for their family and going back home during their annual leave is expected. It is a great time spending your 30 days leave with your family and bond in anyways you want. Go to the beach with your family and friends or go hiking with them. I know that 30 days will never be enough whenever you're with the people you love but we should take these days spending

quality time and building enough memories that are worth remembering.

2. **Travel.** It is one of the best ways to de-stress. Going to different places and new environment is a good way to gain a new perspective and start anew. In fact, we sometimes need to stay away from the common to be able to search for tranquility and detach ourselves from a toxic environment. Take more photos as you've gone from places to places as it would serve as great memories to reminisce while you're sitting on your sofa with your grandchildren in later years. I am sure that there are a lot of websites and travel agencies that offer travel promotion at an affordable cost. I suggest you plan and book ahead of time. That way, it would come in handy for you without compromising a big chunk of money from your wallet.

3. **Engage in Sports or Fitness.** Do you know that sports and fitness activities make us intelligent and remove stress and anxiety? According to *Healthline*, engaging in sports and exercises help stimulate the production of hormones that can enhance the growth of brain cells. Hence, it improves your brain functions and protect your memory and improve your thinking skills. It has been proven that exercises can improve your mood and decrease the feelings of depression, anxiety, and stress. I would also like to add the benefit such as it improves the camaraderie among peers and it promotes sportsmanship. So, if you don't know what you want to do with your vacation leaves, might as well spend it to make your mind and body healthy.

4. **Attend training or enroll in a short course program.** If you are undecided on how to spend your vacation,

you may want to consider enrolling in a short course like baking, or anything that you enjoy doing. It is also a form of de-stressing activity in which you learn, build skills, and at the same time enjoy the pleasure of doing it. This personal development activity is the best way of spending your time especially if you are someone who loves learning for future use. Mind you, time will come that you'll eventually need the skills and knowledge you gained from training and short courses.

5. **Read good books**. Reading improves our mind and imagination that would take us to a different experience. It develops critical thinking, foster imagination, and enhance vocabulary. Through reading, we discover knowledge on printed materials that we can apply in our life or in our career. I could recommend several reading materials, but I'll leave it to you as you have your own preferred genres.

The federal law is very protective of the employees and one that we should take advantage of is the annual leave benefit as mandated. We must spend it wisely and gain the happiness that we deserve because working may sometimes be exhausting. We are always in a battle, a battle of nostalgia while we are away from the people we love if you are one who works abroad. With this, let me borrow a thought from Earl Nightingale, *"Learn to enjoy every minute of your life. Be happy now. Don't wait for something outside of yourself to make you happy in the future. Think how really precious is the time you have to spend, whether it's at work or with your family. Every minute should be enjoyed and savored."*

Bullying in the Workplace: An issue that should never be ignored

DIFFERENT FORMS OF BULLYING AND HOW TO ADDRESS THEM

We cry, and we usually seek for our mother's defense when a bully comes and do something bad. In the world of employment, it is another story. Bullying in all forms needs no introduction and it exists in a way that our senses can be made aware of. For us to understand better, let me define what bullying is in a legal sense. According to **USLEGAL.com,** bullying is generally defined as an intentional act that causes harm to others and may involve verbal harassment, verbal or non-verbal threats, physical assault, stalking, or other methods of coercion such as manipulation, blackmail, or extortion. It is an aggressive behavior that intends to hurt, threaten or frighten another person.

I am sure that there are a lot of instances when an employee is being bullied by his fellow employees, or even by his boss. It comes in different forms that we may not be aware of, or sometimes we choose to ignore. However, this concern is alarming and must be stopped once and for all. I found one good article on different kinds of bullying in office settings. This article is from *Staff Human Resources* of California, U.S.A.

1. **Language or behavior that frightens, humiliates, belittle or degrades a person.** Basically, anything someone says that makes another person feel uncomfortable, ashamed, and offended. This includes the language of insults, aggressive yelling or shouting, unwarranted physical contact or threatening gestures, making repeated negative comments on a person's

appearance lifestyle, family, or culture, inappropriate teasing or pranks, circulating embarrassing photos or videos of a person via email or social media.

2. **Behavior that undermines a person's work performance, working relationships, or perceived value in the workplace may also be part of a pattern of bullying.** One good example that best illustrates this item is when someone is taking credit for someone else's work or contribution. Seemed common right? But that is bullying in all forms, aside from the fact that it is unquestionably unethical.

3. **Maltreatment from a supervisor or manager.** Let me give you a few examples: Establishing unrealistic timelines, or frequently changing deadlines, denying access to information or resources, giving feedback in an insincere or disrespectful manner, repeatedly reminding someone of past errors or mistakes. These are prevalent issues that are happening in the workplace and it is a very terrible thing you could ever experience.

The question on how to cease this appalling circumstance in the office lies on how we react to the situation. Many of us plainly ignore this kind of behavior from colleagues to avoid problems. Some chose to accept the abuse and keep it to themselves, and some stood up against the bullies. What are the things that an employee should do in times like this? How do we manage harassment and bullying in the workplace? We should know that this act is a terminable offense. In the U.A.E., employees are protected by the clause in the labor law particularly in **Article 120 clause 7 and 9** which state that An employer can terminate an employee without prior notice if the worker is finally sentenced by a competent court for an offense involving honor, honesty or public morals; If while working, the worker assaults the employer, the responsible manager, or any of his workmates.

Apart from that, employees should review their company policies and procedures. A lot of us may be wondering why there are bullies and why do they exist? According to **A. Emamzadeh** of the *Psychology Today*, bullies exist because of several reasons which include job insecurities, workload, role conflict or ambiguity. Also, personality factors are the reasons why they exist. Bullies are everywhere, and organizations are not an exemption though it is filled with professionals. They have this distinct characteristic that perhaps a result of their problems back home. The consequence of bullying is severe which include physical and psychological symptoms and negative work-related outcomes such as absenteeism, and that is not good for business. I am sure that the HR department is emphasizing the clause about bullying in the workplace, a grave offense that should be taken seriously. After all, this is something that is out of your mother's control.

Camaraderie in the Workplace

LOOKING THROUGH THE DOORS OF COMPANIONSHIP

What does a workplace become when people inside the company create a harmonious relationship with one another? How does one feel towards work when people inside the organization are ready to lend a hand for you? These are just obvious questions that need not be answered. Social being as we are, we need people in our lives. We need a companion, we need support.

Camaraderie fosters friendship and trust. According to *Christine Riordan* of Harvard Business Review, workers are happier in their jobs when they have friendship with co-workers. Employees report that when they have friends at work, their job is more fun, enjoyable, worthwhile, and satisfying. There are so many things to be valued at work and friends deserve a spot. Business, as we know, is built on trust and its success is dependent on the people working inside the company. When there is a certain level of camaraderie and trust, it is likely that the company will progress. People in the organization will need to be a team working together and develop collusion, trust, friendship, and fun. It is a form of team building in which people get to know each other and support each other. This vibe in the office creates motivation for the employees as they would be comfortable to work with people whom they can trust thus productivity is high. This also fosters healthy competition among the team which makes the company a better place to work for. This will eventually reduce attrition rate.

How a company or team leaders support this kind of activities? Here are just a few suggestions:

1. **Outings** – One of the best things to do especially when you are always stressed out with work. Your team may want to go out for a fun activity such as going on a park or out of town night out. You may ask members to shell out some food for the group or contribute a little amount of money for your outing activity. I am sure that this will bring your team relationship into another level of friendship and harmony.

2. **Travel** – some people love to travel to unwind, well who doesn't? Asking your colleagues for a trip will have a big impact on your comradeship. It could be fun to have them around visiting places and learning new cultures and seeing beautiful sceneries. This leisure activity may be a bit expensive for some so it would be a great idea

to plan for others to prepare. Most of all, make it legal. What I mean is, file for a vacation leave!

3. **Celebrate Birthday or special occasion** – It is good to be recognized especially on your special day. Having a simple celebration in the office will go a long way to making the employee feel special and appreciated. A simple greeting in a post-it or cupcakes for the will have a good effect on one employee. This is important as an employee engagement activity and it builds appreciation, and faith to the company.

4. **Lunch-out** – Going out for lunch is no longer new to some of the employees. But there is more to just go out and eat. This builds companionship and friendship. But when you do, you should do it without spending the entire break on your mobile phone liking other people's posts on Facebook or retweeting another people's tweet. Talk, enjoy, and have fun with the people you're with as the "moment" is more valuable than the food you eat. Don't let social media kill the fun.

5. **Communicate with people** – A simple Hi, Hello, or a smile can do wonders. This no other important things to do that being able to communicate with your colleagues freely and without hesitations. This means that you value being human more than being so tied-up with your job. Humans are social beings and we are not born to just stick our faces in our computers and mobile phones. Again, conversations matter.

I am sure that there are plenty of activities that you can do to develop comradeship in the workplace. It doesn't have to be fancy and expensive. Rather, you can do simple things to make people like one another. As what I have previously said, we need people in our lives. We need them to survive. We need the people in our office for us to have a better place to work.

The effects of Slang in Corporate Communication

SIMPLE ENGLISH FOR OFFICE COMMUNICATION

It is true that the most exciting aspect of English language is its constant evolution. The previous days, I was asked by a friend about the modern slang used by teenagers or the "netizens" nowadays. He threw several words and to my surprise, I didn't have any idea what those words mean. So, since I am bored, I thought, why not do a little more research about this prevalent slang words and how this affects the corporate communication. Here's what I found out:

1. **Miscommunication**. As it is true that the English language is not static, it refreshes over the period of time. But slang slowly dies out along the way. However, this type of communication is acceptable in a certain group of people, certain age, and certain ethnicity. In business, it has a negative effect if constant usage of slang is used. There is no guarantee that business partners and vendors are familiar or understand a certain lingo. This makes communication to be unclear.

2. **Formality is deteriorating**. We all know that slang is an informal language used for verbal communication in an informal situation. However, this does not mean that it must invade the office communication. Corporate communication and business language are far from the language we speak on the streets where you can just use the words you want. Business communication is

important in a way that ideas and words do not die-out as time passes by.

3. **Lack of office engagement.** A group of people in the company uses different words in different functions. It sometimes creates confusion and lack of constant communication within the team or each department. Example, the IT team will talk about *cashed out*, *404*, etc. that accountant may mean a different thing. *Cookie* is a food meant by servers and *cookie* meant differently for IT geeks, knowing that server is also a different thing, not an occupation.

There are so many slangs used by different departments according to their functions and as a result, it is hard to be able to relate to one another. The best cure will be is to familiarize ourselves with occupational or departmentalized slangs. Learning new terminologies will give you a flexibility to communicate with different groups in different situations. After all, language is not dead, it continues to evolve as civilizations continue to improve.

Career Transition: Best ways to handle it

HOW TO COPE WITH THE CHANGES IN YOUR CAREER

We used to dream humongous when we were little. Some dreamed to become a pilot someday. Some wanted to become a doctor, a teacher, a lawyer, and some wanted to become a priest. Of course, those dreams become variables as we grow up. Yes, there are those who are lucky enough to have dreamed as such and ended up doing what they have dreamt about. We get to grow up and we certainly become aware of our surroundings and open our eyes to different interests that the world has prepared for us. We entered the University and took the major that we wished with the vision that we end up doing what we love doing.

We seemed to get a good vision of how our life will look like after we graduate. Trust me, it seemed surreal and magnificent thinking of a comfortable life, earning, and at the same time being in a profession that you desire. Sometimes life directed us towards a path which was entirely different from what we wanted for ourselves. This change affected our line of career and our life itself. Now the question is, how do you cope with this transition?

1. **Acceptance.** We may go through a lot of changes in our lives and it is true that most of the changes are difficult. One way to overcome it is to embrace the change. There's no use in dwelling with the same problem repeatedly because change happens for a reason. You got to get up from your bed, fix yourself, and move on to the next stage of your life. It may not be easy for some but doing so, you are already taking a first step towards moving on. Accept whatever is happening in the course of your career because whether you like it or not, change has just happened.

2. **Make the best out of it.** We may be caught up in a situation where we are placed in the world that is entirely different from where we used to live, and we end up doing something new. It is hard indeed, but we must do our best and turn this event into something beneficial. Take it as a new challenge to better yourself and work hard on it. Just like what people used to say, if you're given a lemon, make a lemonade.

3. **Continue learning.** When changes happen, an opportunity to learn comes in. There is nothing in this world that we cannot learn if we put our heart in it. Just like a new topic in a textbook. We were introduced to the new ideas, and we learn them. Same as with the career transition, it may be challenging but when we put our head and heart to learn new tasks and responsibilities, we'll definitely get the hang of it. It is only a matter of drive and taking ownership that we could learn to be the best version of ourselves.

4. **Trust yourself.** This is the part when you should rely solely on yourself. It is only you who could help yourself better, not someone else. Sometimes, change can be depressing. How much more if this has something to do with your career and something that you really wanted for your life. Trusting yourself comes from the thought within that no matter how hard life is, you will be able to get through it. A determination is a door, and optimism is the key.

5. **Ask for help.** Many of us ignore this stage in our life because we tend to be engulfed by pride that we forget to ask help whenever we needed it. Some are too shy to ask and some just didn't bother. In this transition, it is important to seek help from people who know the job well, or those who have a better understanding of the company's culture. Ask your manager about the tasks that seemed unclear to you as it is better to ask than pretend to know everything. It is by seeking help and guidance that we can learn to do our job well. Ask someone who is senior to you to mentor you. Ask for a training if needed for you to perform better during this transition.

6. **Set your mind towards success.** Acquiring good vibes and setting up your goals for the years to come is one way to do great work. Feel good about yourself and think that you will eventually be successful in your new career. Think that you have no other options but to be successful despite the big change in your career. When you set your mind to your goal, everything else will follow because you will become what you think you will be.

I must agree that change is difficult and that we must pay attention to this problem. It is difficult to adjust especially if you have set your mind on your future plans and have a better view of your life for the years to come. However, a change must not stop us from living. A career change is not a reboot, but it is actually a continuation. It is just a different challenge and a new path to walk on to and a new goal to achieve. A new goal, a fresh perspective. Just like when we used to dream when we were little, to become... someday.

How to Cope with Changes in the Organization

THINGS TO BEAR IN MIND WHEN CHANGES IN THE WORKPLACE OCCUR

Change is one of the constant things in the world. It is inevitable. It is sad sometimes, but it can be fulfilling. It opens different windows of opportunities. This perspective is very dependent on the people's mindset whether he is a pessimist or an optimist. Changes, as we know it, can be worst or best but our emotions and motivations at work get affected. Below are the suggestions on how to cope with it:

1. **Focus your mind on the objective of your work.** This is probably one of the hardest things to do after the management has broken the news that major changes will have to take effect immediately. The news may either be a life changing situation for the employees if you focus your mind on the objective of your work will drive you to perform better. You are there to do your job and deliver good results to your manager of leader. If changes in the workplace are implemented, it is expected of us to work on it not the job itself will work for us.

2. **Embrace the change and make it better.** There is no other way for us to cope with these changes except to embrace it. Whether we like it or not, change is part of the growing business and obsolete practices are scrapped out for modern best practices. Technology is evolving and so the practices, policies, and even the hierarchy in the workplace. If you feel that you cannot cope with it, it is time for you probably to leave or another option is to learn and make it better.

3. **Look for a mentor.** Speaking of learning to love and embrace the change, it is good to look for someone who would help you with the new job or tasks. If change means a new role, look for a colleague who has an idea or is knowledgeable about the job and you should to learn from him. This is one way to be effective and efficient. After all, it is another skill set to learn and an additional value to your credentials as an employee.

4. **Open Communication with your leader or the management.** This is another major thing to do. Communication is an integral part of personal and professional growth. Changes occur around us and it

is right to let people know - especially those who are involved, about how you feel, your motivations, things you need to do, things you need to improve on, and other important factors that are helpful in your job. This way, your manager will have an idea that you are not only responsive to the change but also you are working on it and deliver positive results despite the odds.

It is normal that we feel anxious after the change in the organization, but we can manage our emotions and go through this change. It may be a change of policies like no mobiles allowed during work hours, or no eating in the workstation. It may be a change of tasks or a total revamp of the business cycle. It is always better to assess ourselves and start asking, Can I do these tasks? Can I leave social media behind while at work? Can I work properly without nibbling something crunchy? Do I have the skills to do the job? The above-listed points can be very helpful to cope with the change but at the end of the day, it is us who decide whether to stay or not.

How to handle Rejection on the Promotion that was not Granted?

GRACE AND COMPOSURE AGAINST SOME BAD NEWS

No matter what the scenarios are, it is always disappointing to receive rejection. Especially if that thing that was refused for us is something that you truly deserve and worked hard for. One of the biggest setbacks in the workplace that's demotivating is not giving you the promotion that you should get, nor get the raise that was promised. The question is, how do you handle it? I suggest the below tips to get over with such demotivating news and for you to keep going:

1. **Don't decide anything while you are at the peak of your emotion.** This is the first thing you should do. Relax your mind and decide not to do anything while you are still burning with rage or sadness. Give yourself some time to absorb the news and don't let it cloud your mind to decide something that you may regret in the future. Many of us would immediately decide to hand down our resignation and leave the company because we feel that we don't deserve that kind of treatment, or we feel that our hard work is not recognized. I agree it is very sad and extremely frustrating.

2. **Ask for feedback.** Asking feedback is important. This will be a learning platform to gauge your capacity in doing the job. Your boss has something to say about your performance and so it is just right to ask. This is also a great chance to know what went wrong and the things that you could have done better. Feedback is good when it is given real time.

3. **Continue to do your best.** Once the decision has been made, there's nothing that we could do further because we don't want to beg for something that was refused to us in the first place. Instead, give them your best performance now and the rest of the year. It is the sweet revenge that cultivates nothing but your development, credibility, and worth.

4. **Update your CV.** I am not implying anything, but it is better to prepare for something different. You know what I mean.

Yes, it is hard to accept the fact that sometimes, we feel so little about ourselves because we were not given something that we deserve. However, it is just right to know and make sure that we will not make a wrong move in our career. Let us feed ourselves with the below wisdom:

"The beauty is that through disappointment, you can gain clarity, and with clarity comes conviction and true originality." - Conan O'Brien

How to React and what to do on a Termination Notice

RIGHT WAYS TO HANDLE THIS NOT SO GOOD NEWS

We all have experienced being heartbroken of some sort and there's no immediate remedy to cure this agonizing feeling. However, as time goes by, we get to learn different techniques. Perhaps different ways to make it better. Being heartbroken on a sad news for being terminated from your job is a whole new story. Losing a job is a life-changing scenario in the plot of your career. This is probably one of the news that we avoid receiving and something that we can't afford to have. Different emotions engulf the body and tendencies are, unpleasant reactions occur. So, what are the ways to control our emotions and the best ways to handle this appalling news?

1. **Pause for a moment.** Take your time to absorb the news before reacting because what will come out from our mouth may not be pleasant and can kill our professionalism. Think about it silently, understand, and deal with the emotion later when you're alone. However, if you must ask for some clarifications and of what went wrong, ask politely and with confidence. I know holding back your emotion is not easy but as a professional, we must do our best to make it look easy.

2. **Know when your termination is legal.** Once the notice is served, accept it but don't sign anything right away. Ask for a moment of time to understand the clauses and the content of the letter. Companies cannot terminate employees without valid reasons. It is right to ask for some legal advice from people who are experts when it comes to labor laws. Do not go ballistic. Instead, keep your cool.

3. **Keep your dignity.** According to *Lea McLeod, M.A.*, begging to keep your job will never change the manager's mind. So, keep your dignity intact and focus on the rest of your conversation. It is time to raise your questions if you have, ask for some valid documentation and answers as to why they result to terminate your employment. Begging and crying in front of the manager will just give a bad impression to you as a professional. Straight conversation and queries can aid better understanding between the two parties.

4. **Say "Thank you" anyway.** This is a professional way of acknowledging the management's decision. After you know that there's nothing more you could do, just say thank you and go on doing the remaining tasks that you have for a better hand-over. But don't force yourself from working too hard while you're are at the verge of your emotion. You will just end up being inefficient. Always bear in mind that there are still a lot of things to be thankful for. For one, the opportunity to experience working in that kind of environment, the chance to meet people, and more.

5. **Ask for the computation of your final settlement.** Check all the details of your final pay. Make sure you have all the information on your benefits, from the

unused leave computation, gratuity, and others that you are entitled to. Check them and understand every detail. Ask if you must but never rush signing anything.

Losing a job is not easy and some of us may be able to relate to it. But this does not mean we should deal with it again and again. Make it a reason to do better and find a perfect organization to work for. The world is vast and full of opportunities for people who never stop dreaming, working, and believing in themselves. We live a life that heartbreaks in different forms exist, but life continues for people who never give up. Let us feed out thoughts with this wonderful quote, *"Never give up. Today is hard, tomorrow will be worse, but the day after will be sunshine."* – **Jack Ma.**

Things to Remember before Resigning

A PRACTICAL GUIDE IN MAKING A DECISION ON RESIGNATION

As they say, leaving the company is one of hardest things to do especially if you've grown to like your colleagues, the culture, and the environment. To some, it may mean a sigh of relief to finally get out of the ugly situation in the office. No matter what your reasons are, you should always bear in mind the below things before you decide sending your resignation letter to your boss:

1. **Think not just once or twice, but multiple times.** I know that this might sound a cliché, but it is important that resignation needs to be thought of multiple times. This kind of decision will affect not only your career but also your personal life. Ask the opinion of your closest friends or a family member before jumping under the

bus because it is always worth it to hear the opinion, and perhaps the guidance of others.

2. **Make sure you have another company to work for.** If you are someone who cannot afford to be vacant even just for a month or two, then this is for you. Make sure you already have attended interviews and a job offer has already been signed before you tend your resignation to your boss. This will make sure that you have a worry-less departing from your current company. We all know how hard it is to find a job especially in today's market situation where there is a talent competition going on and a shaky market condition. The 30-day extension after the cancellation of your residence visa feels like yesterday when the opportunity is not in your favor.

3. **Make sure you're aware of the kind of company you're going to.** It doesn't make sense to just leave and jump to another company without some good knowledge of the organization you're going to. Make sure that you know the company's culture, it's financial stability and the working environment. I am sure that there are lots of ways to get this information. Make sure it is the right choice, and that you'll be happy. It pays to be knowledgeable and foresee the kind of life you're living with your new company. Otherwise, you'll see yourself updating your CV and sending hundreds of applications AGAIN.

4. **Clear all your dues and financial obligations in your company.** This is just the right thing to do. This matter is one of the reasons why some employees find it hard to leave the company simply because they are still tied up with some financial obligations. Settle them first before resigning because your end of service benefit could help

a lot in your transition rather than having it deducted from your dues and you end up receiving nothing.

5. **Make sure you have enough fund in your accounts.** This probably one of the most important things to remember. You need to have enough money to pay off your housing bills, travel allowances, and food while you're still waiting for your next salary. We all know that things can get expensive if you don't have enough resources. Your end of service benefit takes a while before it will come into your bank account. Sometimes it takes a month or two before you receive it.

There's really no way to predict the future. All we could do is to arm ourselves with knowledge and enough preparations for what will come. This practical guide may help us in making a smooth transition and worry-free career leap should we decide to leave our current company. We may differ with reasons as to why we resign, it doesn't matter for a long as we take precautions and only then we can somehow make sure that leaving comes easy.

Reasons why People keep Jumping from one Job to Another

THE IMPORTANCE OF SETTING A CAREER GOAL

Jumping from one company to another is no longer surprising as it all comes down to what one really wants career-wise. Many of us don't exactly know what seems to be the right fit and understand what works best. That is the importance of having a career goal. One might say that why don't we just have to go with the flow and see what will happen? That is probably what everybody is thinking – to just go with the flow and wait what life leads you. However, going with the flow may not always what we need especially if you're talking about the crucial part of development to have a successful career. The below are the examples of the things that must be done differently.

1. **Not assessing yourself.** It is important that as a person, we know our capabilities and strength. We should know ourselves better – from the skill sets we stand-out up to our potentials. This is very helpful when it comes to set our goals in life and career. At least we know what we are fighting for, and we know the right tools to use for the battles.

2. **Do not set realistic goals.** Setting a realistic goal is paramount to success. Make sure that is achievable in a certain period of time, whether it is a long-term or short-term goal. When you have a goal in mind, you are focused on what you need to do to achieve those goals hence, it prevents you from a career deviation. But remember that this happens only if you already know what you want in life.

3. **Do not set measurable goals.** Plans and goals need to be measurable. Make sure to have a list of your plans and goals in a spreadsheet and check whether it has achieved or not. Make a timeframe of each goal and track them. That way, you'll be able to know what needs to do next and what needs to be done to achieve the goals in the list. It is important to do it one by one but sure steps towards achieving all those. If one does not have a measurable goal, it is likely that he will end up switching to different areas of interests and jump to another company to start all over again.

4. **Pessimism.** According to *Dawn Mckay* of The Balance Career, your goal should be something that you want, not something you want to avoid. Sometimes, we are too concentrated on the things that we shouldn't have rather than the things we should look forward to. We tend to grow tired of waiting and as a result, we decide impulsively to look for a differ job. If you think you can't be qualified for the promotion that you aim for, there are still things that you should do to achieve it. For one, develop your skills by attending training or enrolling in courses that will elevate your learnings and abilities. Don't let negative thoughts drive your career to the endpoint.

5. **Lack of actions.** Plans are nothing without action. What you do is imperative to the realization of your goals. Make sure that those actions are little steps towards your aim. When learning opportunity comes, which you think is essential for your development and plans, then go for it. It is like taking actions and doing what's necessary. There are some whose plans are superb, but they did different things and ended up frustrated for having been striding a different path.

6. **Do not envision the plans.** This is a failure of many, not having the right mind to visualize success. For you to keep on the right track, you should always maintain a vision of success that you really want. When you stop visualizing, you'll lose the drive and the fire of determination within you. Remember, you become what you think you'll become and that's a great mindset. Not many people have it and when you set a goal, create an imagery of the future you and how it feels have what you really want in life. This will serve not only an inspiration but a guide towards success.

To sum it all up, having a career goal and knowing how to set them right are crucial to success. Knowing yourself and the things you want will be the guiding point of it all. Back them up with the right actions, optimism, and vision of success. They are the right mixtures of a fulfilling and goal-oriented career.

Why Employee Empowerment Vital for Organizational Success?

HOW TO EMPOWER EMPLOYEES TO ACHIEVE ORGANIZATIONAL GOALS?

Employees are the bloodline of the organization and it is true that it can't function without these hardworking individuals who run our business. Empowering our employees can come a long way in attaining great success in the organization. As there are a lot of reason in empowerment, there will be a lot of things to do. How do we empower our employees? Below is the list I gathered which I think is important for us to consider.

1. **Establish trust** - Trust is earned as what the cliché saying goes. Giving your employees the autonomy to do his job on his own rules and ways demonstrate trust. It is one way to loosen up the traditional method of making your employees. Working without looking at the scrupulous list of rules is a good feeling. This could be a great idea to break the uptight culture especially for millennials.

2. **Involve your employees in decision making** – young generation nowadays love to be heard and asked their input about the projects or with regards to the tasks at hand. There's no better way to value your employees than to ask them their input and opinion. It matters to them and it boosts their confidence to do more.

3. **Train and mentor employees** – Learning and developing talents are more important than getting a pay check every month. Advancing employee's skills are rewarding at it develops their knowledge and capabilities in performing their job. As a result, employees feel appreciated and empowered with knowledge. Having someone to mentor them is a great way to make them feel valued and well taken care of.

4. **Set rewards not punishments** – There are people who can't handle punishments and most likely, they ended up demotivated. Rewards could change the employees' perspective towards the kind of job they have because it will give them the honor, confidence, and motivation. A tap in the back, an email announcement, a congratulatory announcement on the board, and an extended vacation, to name a few, could come a long way to make your employees appreciated and empowered.

5. **Flexible working hours** – This has been a trend in Human resources as an alternative to making a productive and stress-free working environment for employees. True enough, it is also one way of saying, *"You are responsible for taking your time, at the same time delivering expected results."* This could mean that you are giving your employees responsibilities, not just tasks to accomplish.

I am sure that the list goes on. It is up for the organization to be creative in encouraging, rather than imposing rules for the employees. We can never see results if we won't take the chance to give what is best to our employees and take the risks in making this happen.

PERSONALITY DEVELOPMENT

Chapter 3

CREATING A BETTER VERSION OF OURSELVES

In this chapter, articles on personality development are highlighted which will give a lot of very specific and practical guidelines and tips to become a better professional, not only in the corporate arena, but also as a professional in all industries. This includes proper ways of communication and creating a better version of ourselves.

"What we need to *succeed* is not what is right in front of us. It is what inside of our head – ideas, passion, and optimism."

How to Leave Good Impression that Lasts

TIPS FOR ESTABLISHING YOURSELF A WINNING CHARACTER

In wherever part of the world you may be at, attitude really counts a lot before anybody else will generate judgment on you. People see and judge you in an instant and it's up to you on how you make others formulate a good impression on you. Below are the things that you may want to consider if you wanted to make good impressions to your colleagues or acquaintance:

1. **Be proactive.** In the workplace, being proactive to the tasks will make quite an impact to your supervisor and colleagues. It says a lot about your character and a well-established work ethics that your supervisor or manager will not regret for hiring you. It is a game of diligence and rich values at work.

2. **Smile.** Don't fake it because people will see it in your eyes. Smile lightens up someone's day even those who struggles a lot. It is a powerful tool in making people like you as it generates positive vibes and a welcoming presence. It exudes positive energy that the people need. Added to the list, drawing a smile on your face gives people the idea that you are an approachable person and that it won't be hard to trust you.

3. **Greet genuinely.** A simple hello or a good morning to people won't hurt. It tells so much about your character that you are a person who's polite and cares about the humanity. Being so passive to your colleagues or to people around you make the environment toxic as it

drags the good ambiance down to its zero point of a friendly zone.

4. **Communicate regularly.** Communication is vital in every situation. It promotes avoidance of any conflict that may arise. Constant communication with your colleagues or manager speaks something about you being conversant enough to know something that would make you a better person. Moreover, it creates camaraderie among your colleagues and it is a good way to make you a likable person.

5. **Speak truthfully.** Integrity in the workplace is something that is badly needed from all. One of the requirements to achieve such integrity is by speaking truthfully in every communication you have, be in in writing or speaking. You are doing the right thing even when no one is looking. It is the ultimate behavior that radiates from our inner self which makes us a better person as a result.

These simple acts require no training and should be coming from our selves. Behaviors such as these are basic things to consider yet will make a person likable and trusted. Being yourself is a good way to build connection with others especially in the officer. But being oneself sometimes can be look at a different angle and that can be subjected to misinterpretations. No one is the same and we all differ in personalities and beliefs. Make sure to always look at the good things and not the other way around because you will end up less likable.

Stress Management: Combating stress towards achieving targets

A big factor why people leave their job is because of the stress at work. It is the invisible culprit that stings the minds of people and bring them down. There are many ways to challenge this in taking the precautions to combat this one thing that hinders you from performing. Below are the simple suggestions to eliminate the stress at work:

1. **Avoid being a perfectionist**. There goes a cliché saying that nobody is perfect. True enough, this will just lead you to a burnout at the end of the day. We cannot expect people in tour team to be perfect and work flawlessly all the time. When you are trying to be perfect, chances are, you cannot live life to the fullest and that means you deprive yourself the challenge and surprises of life. You'll end up depressed over little things that sometimes takes time to achieve. Perfectionists believe that there is no room for mistakes and that is unhealthy especially in the workplace.

2. **Set your goals one at a time.** It is good when you know how to multi-task. But do you know that it harms your mind? **Dr. Travis Bradberry** of *TalentSmart* said that multitasking damages your brain and that it lowers IQ. These were proven through research from the University of Sussex. They have found out that high multitaskers had less brain density in the anterior cingulate cortex, a region responsible for empathy as well as cognitive and emotional control. Having said that, when your mind focused on multiple tasks gives you the disadvantage to performing better. Scatterbrain will add up to you being emotionally and intellectually stressed. Set your goals one at a time, prepare a checklist of the things that you

need to do, tick those you have completed and jump to the next one. It is one way to organize your job and it makes your brain healthy.

3. **Ignore toxic people.** There's always an undeniable presence of toxic people in every organization, and how we deal with them affects our behavior and performance at work. Toxic people are hard to deal with. They extract every energy in your body and will give you nothing but stress and unhealthy environment. If you want to perform better at work, distant yourself from this kind of people. Sometimes, there are ways to handle this kind of people. You just have to find out.

4. **Get enough sleep.** Prior to going to work, you should get enough and a good night sleep. It will give you enough energy and good feeling at work. Enough sleep will generate cells in your body and will make you feel alive the next day. It is hard to concentrate at work when you are sleepy and that means the quality of work is compromised.

5. **Get some exercise.** Exercise will bring more benefits as it is one way to stay healthy. A healthy body is a healthy mind. Sweat out the stress away and it will make you feel good. When inside the office, it is recommended to stretch your body every 2 hours to let the blood flow freely. Twist your body and arms simultaneously, blink your eyes several times, and take a deep breath. Also, take a short break every 15 minutes especially if your work requires you to stay in front of your computer all day.

6. **Drink plenty of water.** Water gives a lot of benefits in our body. It neutralizes our body temperature. When

feeling a little fatigue, drink a glass of water and it will make you feel relaxed. It is said *(Amanda Carlson, MS, RD, CSSD)* that when being dehydrated for half a liter increases your cortisol level in your body. That cortisol is one of the stress hormones, and I'm sure you don't want that. All your organs in the body, including your brain, require water to function well.

A healthy lifestyle at work is something that we need to prioritize. We work to earn, or to achieve simple pleasures in life. An effective stress management at work would elevate employee's performance and that is needed for a better career. There's no good at stress. It is something that we can control and avoid once and for all because they would bring us down, considering the psychological effects it can give us. Be stress-free, it will give you joy!

How to Maintain Productivity at Work

EMPLOYEE'S DOSAGE TO YIELD EXCELLENT RESULTS IN THE WORKPLACE

It may be true that many of us are guilty at some point doing nothing or we are just being busy procrastinating. Being unproductive also means having a lot of things on our plate but not knowing which one to start. Our work can be measured at some point when it comes to the quality of the work done. However, it is imminent that these scenarios are prevalent in the office. How do we maintain being productive even though we have nothing to do? Please look and consider the suggested tips:

1. **Avoid procrastination** – Guilty! Most of us, if not all, are guilty about this. Procrastination is the enemy of

productivity. Leaving tasks for tomorrow that could have been done today is not a good practice at work. You would be surprised of the never-ending piles of papers on your desk.

2. **Set priorities and manage your tasks** – setting up priorities in your list is a good idea especially when you're beating the deadline. Start with the most important down to the least ones or ad hocs when necessary. Do not just employ a multi-tasking strategy as it may result to cramming and inefficient results. As what **Dr. Travis Bradberry** said, multi-tasking is damaging our brain, and decreases the quality of your work. Accomplishing our tasks step by step and one at a time will give us a quality work.

3. **Take a break from time to time** – Taking breaks is healthy. It will refresh our minds when we go back to doing our tasks. Fresh minds can do wonder. It will set our mood into a restart and will give us a good understanding, perspective, and energy at work. When we set our priorities well, taking a break does not hurt our time and good results will follow.

4. **Ask questions for something that you don't know** – There is no point doing things that you have no idea about. It will just consume your energy for something that is unproductive and useless by the end of the day. It is encouraged to ask someone on how to do things than pretend you know something that you don't. Go straight to the point and ask your boss or a colleague on how to do certain task properly for efficient results. In that way, you don't have to repeat if you get it the first time.

5. **Read articles and new information** – I know that reading for some, isn't their cup of tea. For some, this is time consuming or a boring stuff to do while inside the office. However, if tasks are done, reading some good stuff such as articles and informative write-ups will make us smarter and well-informed. I suggest reading at least one or two articles a day which are related to your line of work or those that are related to your company industry. This will give you updated information and knowledge to do better in your job hence, not a waste of time at all.

As an employee, it is inevitable to feel lazy at times but once you are dedicated in your work, you can surpass the challenge of boredom or cramming. Whatever ways you wanted to spend your time in the office, make sure to get the best value of your time without compromising the result of your work. As what John F. Kennedy said, *"We must use time as a tool, not as a crutch."*

Suggestions on How to Expand your Vocabulary

TECHNIQUES USED TO UNCOVER THE HIDDEN AND UNFAMILIAR WORDS

You may wonder why some people are fluent in both spoken and written English with a very distinct and accurate word use. They are those who know many words in the dictionary and that sounds smart, right? Let me tell you this, having a broad vocabulary gives you an advantage in academic and professional facets. How do we fish words from the wide ocean of English language? Below are the suggested tips and techniques:

1. **Read, read, and keep on reading!** This is a great way of learning. You'll encounter words that seemed to be unfamiliar to you, I suggest you look the meaning up in the dictionary. The English language has a lot of words to offer and reading is a way to grab them. It is like finding treasure in every stage of the race. You can find many unfamiliar words from literature such novels and short stories, and some from the articles online. They are the bank of unfamiliar words. Today, many resources are available such as internet which is available 24/7.

2. **Keep a note of every word you encounter.** Words are everywhere, you'll probably get a chance of meeting them while you travel, on the sign boards, fliers, and leaflets, or you probably eavesdropped from the people inside the bus or train. Be ready to take your pen and notebook with you and scribble the words that you don't know. Don't mind the spelling first, the online dictionary will help you find it because google is amazing. It will give you suggested words if you don't get it right the first time.

3. **Take online English vocabulary test.** This is a fun way to widen your vocabulary. In this digital age, there are a lot of applications that provide you with various educational games such as vocabulary tests. What is amazing about it is that it will give you the chance to see the unfamiliar words and give you the meaning and answer after the test. Try the Webster dictionary app, it has a game as such.

4. **Visit online dictionary and thesaurus.** This is an amazing technique to know more words in a day. These online sources present new words every day and I'm sure you want to take note if you wanted to have a

wide vocabulary. Thesaurus is also one good source. It will give you synonyms and antonyms of the words that you can use in writing. However, make sure that the word you are trying to use must be in the right context with your thought and meaning. Again, check both dictionary and thesaurus to make sure.

5. **Watch English movies and listen how the words are being pronounced**. It is an exercise and perhaps fishing with the words that may sound strange to you. Again, repeat the cycle, search the meaning and try to check its synonyms and antonyms for better understanding.

6. **Use them every day!** This is by far the most important part. You should use the words you know in every conversation or emails you will send. With constant use of the words, the better retention it will be. It is useless if you know the words and you'll keep then hidden. Tendencies are, it will be forgotten. Converse with your friends. It is a good way to practice your speaking skills as well.

In academic and formal writing situation, it is better not to use the same words in the same sentence. There are various sources that we could check on to replace redundant and overused words. English has diverse sets of terminologies that we can use in a sentence. It is recommended that we make full use of these resources and techniques to expand our vocabulary for better writing and speaking skills.

5 Important Things that a Great Public Speaker Should Possess

UNLEASHING YOUR POTENTIALS FOR GREAT SPEAKING ENGAGEMENTS

It takes great effort and experience to become an effective public speaker. There are no tricks nor some sort of magic that would make a person a great speaker in an instant. Continuous toil, and perhaps the right amount of experience would make one better. However, what really are the things that a great public speaker should possess? Below is a list of things that would make a person great at doing talks in front of the public:

1. **Credibility.** This is very important among the things that a speaker should possess, and it is the hardest one to get as well. Credibility means the capacity to bring the information to a higher level of truthfulness. It is showing your audience that you are speaking in a manner which a considerable amount of honesty and integrity are put together. Example, using your own product and experience the result before talking in front of your potential customers is an example of credibility. Being credible is like being reliable. Using your beauty products that you are trying to sell is another example. Presenting a thesis that you researched yourself is another one. With all these examples, a speaker would find it easy to explain, convey, and communicate his ideas to his audience because he experienced it first-hand.

2. **Confidence.** It takes a lot of efforts and practice to be confident. Some say it is an innate ability of a person, but some say it can be developed. Confidence is exactly what a speaker needs right there on stage. It is the very

center of success because all the brilliant information and smart ideas are nothing if they are delivered by a timid and shy person. Confidence is what it takes to be successful in every conference and talk. This nerve-wracking activity is absolutely not for everybody. Only those who grow confidence in them to be able to break the center stage and influence others.

3. **Communication skills.** Exceptional communication skills are needed to attain the greatest height in a public speaking engagement. In communication, the way you convey your message matters. It is not just the content, but the pronunciation, delivery, diction, and non-verbal cues are important as well. They are the spices that make a speaker great.

4. **Humor.** The attention span of every individual does not last long especially in a cozy and comfortable venue for a two or three-hour speaking engagements. Humor is specifically tailored by the speakers to capture the attention of the listeners. It is a great way to keep them engaged and focused on the discussion. Cracking humorous jokes or coming up with a funny statement is difficult at some point because not all the people listening could relate. Jokes must be culturally accepted, and the familiarity of the language affects the effectiveness of humor behind the words. Therefore, it takes an intelligent and smart man to make people laugh at the same time engaged in a discussion.

5. **Charm.** Having this kind of personality helps to be a great speaker. This means that you possess a desirable trait of an agreeable and charismatic person. How to become a charismatic person? Well, it can't be taught. It is a combination of all good qualities of a person such

as confidence, truthfulness, kindness, active listener, intelligence, and being a people person.

While it is true that some of us are gifted with the public speaking skills, some become effective after a numerous training and experience. Standing up for what you believe in and share to the public is indeed a privilege that not all are given the chance. The above-listed things provide us an avenue and a chance to be a great public speaker that we desire.

6 Tips to Consider in Speaking before the Crowd

A PUBLIC SPEAKING GUIDELINES FOR ALL OCCASIONS

Speaking in front of the crowd is a communication skill that is indeed a moment for one to inform, influence, and inspire others. Perhaps half of the world no longer reads to be informed but most of them listen instead. Effective public speaking skills are needed for one to do all these reasons and so, I have come up with a helpful list to consider before speaking in front of the crowd.

1. **Research.** I know that some of you may be aware of the part in which people will ask questions after the speech or presentation. I am sure you don't want to look ludicrous in front of your audience when asked something that you don't know. Having said that, it is important to back up your knowledge by doing some research prior to giving a talk. Make sure that you have substantial amount of research that would validate the information you're giving. Audience seeks for substance, and knowledge is what you will share and that should be credible through the right sources and measures.

2. **Review your speech.** In writing, it is important that you must read it multiple times to make sure that you spot all the errors. This is important because being a speaker, people look at you as an intellectual human being with the power to influence and to do business with. So, the content of your speech should be flawless, and it means without grammar errors, inappropriate word choice, and the like. A well written speech is as strong as a hypnotism in an immediate basis. Sometimes, it is hard to spot errors by yourself. Ask someone to do it for you, perhaps someone who is knowledgeable enough to make such corrections.

3. **Back-up plan.** It is advisable to have a back-up plan for all the things that you will present. It is a prevention that is better than cure. Materials that you will use in presenting during your talk contribute to the development of the over-all performance and success. These materials may be your power point presentation, video clips, and any other forms of audio-visual tools. Having a back-up plan does not necessarily mean that you forecast an epic fail of your materials but who knows? These technologies can be affected by any other forces that would make them malfunction and vulnerable. Back-up plan is one way for you to be always ready in case of inevitable technical problems. We are being provided with a lot of devices to store our presentations and materials to such as hard drives, pen drives, and cloud technologies. They are all within reach and it does not hurt to take time to save our work in different forms of storage devices. Be smart!

4. **Practice.** Well, this may be overrated but it is true. If you want to have perfection in everything you do, constant practice is the key. There are things that you may notice

about yourself when you practice in front of the mirror or tape your voice in a recording machine. You may notice some odd gestures that you must not do when speaking or notice a high pitch of your voice which is unnecessary. These are major things for you to consider in delivering your speech as they help you convey the message effectively. Practice before the talk is very important. It gives you the time to evaluate yourself if there are things that you need to improve on, and if there are things that you need to change or do more.

5. **Arrive early.** The essentials of being punctual are often ignored by many. In public speaking, it is crucial to come to the place early to make sure that you have the "feel" of the stage and the proximity. This would make you comfortable and prevent being overwhelmed with the surroundings. You'll get the chance to do your blockings on stage where you want to go to in whichever part of your speech that is appropriate. Stand on the stage and pretend that you've been there several times and that you are the master of the center stage. This will boost your confidence and will help you be at ease during the delivery.

6. **Take a deep breath.** Before going to the stage, make sure to take a deep breath as it will make you feel relaxed and ready. Crack your knuckles and stretch out back stage. Your nerves will loosen up and it will make you comfortable. Bit your lips and massage your face. These tips are helpful especially to those who always fell nervous.

Conor Neill of Forbes said that the ability to speak in front of the public will bring you more opportunities in life. Well, he is correct. The ability to speak in front of the crowd takes more than just a gut – it takes skills and bravery. Those skills probably are the most wanted skills especially in the field of business. Most of us feel anxious about it but with the right aid of the information presented above, we can always overcome the fear of the unknown.

6 Essential Phrases and Sentences used by Great Leaders

LEADERSHIP AT ITS BEST

Being a leader is not just learned within a time frame, but it is acquired through experience and a continuous learning process. It is an essential skill of a person who stands out among the rest of us who are involved in the business. They are the people who put their best foot forward to be able to influence, inspire, and touch other's lives and create a purpose. Leadership comes in different situations and in different places. The question is, what really defines a leader? What are his ways and how does he deal with his subordinates? It comes down to one of the most important part – his words. Below are the examples of phrases that a good leader use:

1. *"Let's do it."* Powerful isn't it? A leader use "us" instead of "you". He always involves himself in the process to doing the tasks of the entire team. This differentiate the leader from a boss. He does not dictate, and he does not force. Instead, he encourages.

2. *"It would be better if… What do you think?"* Now this is encouraging and engaging. Employees are motivated to do their job once they are engaged in decision making especially if this is a work of a team. It is strange, but a leader consults his subordinates. Having them involved

in a conversation and asking their opinion about something give them an impression that they matter.

3. *"You're doing a great job."* A simple pat in the back is good but couple it with this kind of commendation feels like you created a major impact to the development of the team. It is a silent encouragement for them to do better and at the same time, it is a loud applause that they would ever hear.

4. *"Thank you."* The word of magic is not only limited to abracadabra or those words uttered in Harry Potter series but the simple *thank you* are magic words that live through the heart of individual. It is inspiring in a sense that this simple actuation brings light and good aura to the life of the people around you. It is a simple word of gratitude that illuminates positive vibes and good demeanor in the workplace.

5. *"I'm sorry."* Now, this may be the hardest thing to say among leaders. However, a true leader knows how to accept faults and ask for apology to the person he wronged. It takes courage to accept the reality that sometimes we make mistakes. What makes it hard for some is the fact that they are in the higher seat. So, saying sorry does not kill. It does not make you less a leader if you're doing that. In fact, people will look up to you because you are brave in accepting your faults.

6. *"It's okay...We'll make it better the next time."* Admit it or not, failure is part of growth and it is part of life. In the workplace, we just don't enjoy the glory of success, but time comes that failures get in the way to shake us. A leader must know how to pacify and make things right for his underlying employees. Saying these

words not only gives the people a positive outlook and determination, but also a real support which is very important for them. This says a lot towards the attitude that mistakes happen but making it right the second time around makes it different. A true leader is ready to accept defeat, and brave enough to stand lead.

As what *Melisa McLeod* said, the words of the leader matter. Indeed, he has the power to not only influence but also to inspire others to do better in becoming an effective employee. Remember that as a leader, you are their second guardian aside from their parents because they look up to you. So, the above sentences that effective leaders use are just some of the examples that you may want to consider especially if you are a leader or an aspirant one.

Reading: A Habit worth the Expense of Time

READING AND ITS BENEFITS

In this kaleidoscopic world, many of us are trying to cope with the changes that occur around us. Technology, culture, beliefs, to name a few, are the examples why people must be fully aware and be in line with the changes. For us to become in line with our society, one must be informed not only in the field of Science and Technology, but also in all aspects of human existence. There are many ways for us to be informed but for me, the most effective way is reading. We spend most of our time reading. We may not be aware of such but if you look and notice, you have been reading signs, symbols, words, instructions, and other stuff all day. The information we get out of those reading materials are helpful ways to develop our mental capacity. It is true that we can also acquire information through attending symposiums or other public speaking engagement. But if you really must view the whole perspective, presenters or speakers prepared visual aids for his audience to read. For the audience to be fully informed, they will have to read the presentation. We now are being bombarded with technological advancement, social media is an influential example of ways to be informed. We communicate through posting our status or sending personal messages through Facebook and Instagram or through skype, twitters, and emails, and we read them for sure.

College students read not only because they are required to do so but also it is an essential part of being a student. It is essential in a way that most of the lectures and assignments given are done through reading. To survive in the competitive world of university, one must read. In fact, to answer the questions given in the examinations, we should read. In whatever fields we are in, various reading materials are prepared to enlighten us more with the topic. It is one way to feed our minds with various updated forms of wisdom that we could apply as we face the world. Intellectual nourishment is easy to attain if we read in advance because not everything is spoon fed to us by our professors or mentors. Technically, we can expand our knowledge by having a bunch of reading. Learning is infinite and so the information. It is up to us on how to chase them and absorb them in our being.

Several technical reading materials are right in front of us but there are also large percentage of people who read for pleasure. These reading materials perhaps, are in the form of literature. There are different genres of literature people read. It might be novels, short stories, poetries, epics, and others. These forms of literature can give us not only the information we need that happened in the past, but also the awareness of different cultures and traditions around the world. The art of writing is involved in publishing huge amount of materials and so authors have mirrored the cultures into their master pieces. Aesthetic wise, authors intend readers to be imaginative with a pinch of emotion. Novels for examples are written to make the readers cry, laugh, hate, fall in love, and others. Most importantly, reading literature will enhance our critical thinking and sound judgment. As depicted in the story, authors may provide situation in which the reader has to imagine and give out his ideas about what's going on. Reading these will absolutely take you to different places around the world simply because ethnic and tribes of different counties have very rich in literature and have a whole bunch of stories to tell. Reading these materials is like going to a certain place itself. For me, if people find pleasure in reading, he attains the highest fulfillment of all for it is not easy. It needs full attention or focus, patience, and time. Without these, you may not be called voracious reader.

Now, reading as we know it has provided us a lot of advantages and personal development and I couldn't think of any misfortune or disadvantage of reading. Perhaps, it all depends on individual perspective on how reading can give them an absolute advantage. As I have mentioned, learning is infinite so as the information. It is up to us to chase them by reading or not.

11 Tips for Writing a Professional Email

EMAIL WRITING ETIQUETTE IN BUSINESS SETTINGS

Electronic mail or email makes communication easy with the business in the organization. Emailing is a vital activity of the professionals to communicate, express, inform, and influence a person or a group of people. That is the reason why there should be a proper way of making your email look strong and professional. Have a glimpse at the below tips in making your email readable and professionally convincing:

1. **Avoid Jargon.** Make sure that your words are easily understood by your readers.
   Jargons and industry languages are good only for those who are familiar with it. However; when sending a general message to colleagues or clients, leave no room for jargons as they hinder the understandability of your message.

2. **Be direct to the point.** Directness is the key to effectively convey your ideas or messages to another person. Do not beat around the bush, use simple sentences instead. Remember, one sentence, one idea. Professionals are busy people and they don't have time to read your long explanation in one email.

3. **Use simple Language.** Emailing is not the time to showcase the high-sounding words you know or those figurative sentences you have been using in normal conversation. Use simple language or words that are easy to understand. Always remember your purpose in sending an email. Do you need your receiver to have a full understanding of what you are trying to say? So, start using simple words because it does not make you look like a less educated person. There are places where you could put your knowledge on grandiloquent words, but not in a professional email. You write to express, not to impress.

4. **Use short and catchy subject.** The use of short subject line is essential if you don't want to have your message get into people's junk emails. A short subject line makes

it easier to read and easier to understand. Add a little touch of a catchy phrase to make sure that your email is read. This is important among sales professionals who would like to assert a certain proposal. Let us not forget that sometimes, professionals are caught up with their busy tasks and that they ignore emails. Having a catchy and interesting subject line which is related to your content, make them itch to open your message.

5. **Avoid using different font styles and sizes.** Having said that, I mean consistency with the kind of word style you will use in writing your email. It does not look good when some of your words appear bigger than the rest and not pleasing to the eyes neither. Be consistent. Use only one size and style all throughout. Internet and devices, or whatever they call it could detect malware or virus templates such as the ones you write with different styles, sizes, and colors and could end up in the trash.

6. **Use professional tone.** In writing, readers could hear your voice and that means we should sound professional in whatever purpose you're sending an email for. It is by the choice of words that you may sound polite. Add to the list the use of magic words whenever necessary. It is advisable not to write or reply when you are emotional because a person tends to be outrageous and has a high tendency to write profane words. Avoid that once and for all because your words reflect how professional you are. By the end of the day, you have the reputation to keep. In some cases, such as writing complaint letters, be firm but still choose to be professional. It does not hurt to be nice.

7. **Personalize your email.** This is very easy to do. Own your email and do not copy-paste it from the internet

or from the template. It means creating it with your own words and addressing your recipient by their first name. However, be careful in addressing them by their first name because some professionals would like to be addressed as Dr., Professor, Mrs., Mr., etc. It is always best to ask them first. Personalizing your email has the power to influence the mind of your reader because they know it is a human being who writes them an email and not an electronic device that uses templates and auto-response email.

8. **Use bullet points.** One way to organize your thoughts in a trail of email is by using bullet points. They are very helpful especially if you wanted to highlight important points or considerations. Other than that, it will make your email less compact and it contributes to the readability of your message. Your reader would appreciate it especially if you are pointing out important information in a form of bullets as it is easy for them to see it immediately.

9. **Avoid emoticons.** Professionally written documents and emails do not have emoticons. Simply because your words serve as an emotion to your content and that there is no need for you to add these hilarious emoticons in your email. They just aren't professional to look at and they do not reflect much of a need and purpose in your documents. Don't be too emotional!

10. **Check your grammar before sending.** Well, I must say that I sometimes am guilty with this. It really pays off if you review your email before sending because it will give you the chance to correct your grammar, spelling, punctuations, etc. English-wise, it is very important

for you to have an errorless email as it mirrors your professionalism as an employee.

11. **Check attachments.** This is one of the downfalls of many. I understand that most of you are quite busy, but when sending an email, take the time to review the attachment if you attached the documents successfully. Apart from that, make sure you attached the correct one!

Email indeed became a big part of our professional life. They make us a better employee, better boss, or a better customer. Sometimes, the success and answers that we need to get from the people we want to deal business with, rely on how well we understand and compose a message. The above things are the simple things to follow in composing an email for whatever purposes you may have.

8 Suggestions for Effective Study Habits

TIPS AND INKLINGS FOR USEFUL ACADEMIC WORKS AND HABITS

Studying is part of life and it is one thing that students feel awful about. For some, nothing is easier than just sit down in front of the lecture and day dream about your future and even plans for the day. However, thinking about your future without a degree begets a painful result. Mind you, it is not easy to survive in college but if you'll think about ways and reasons to go on, everything will come in handy. Below are just some tips and study habits for one to effectively ace the exams:

1. **Have enough sleep.** This is an important activity for our brain. According to *J. Peever et al.*, sleep serves to

reenergize the body's cells, clear waste from the brain, and support learning and memory. Now it explains why people who have a good night sleep perform better at school than those who deprive themselves in getting enough sleep. It is hard to concentrate in the discussion when you are sleepy because our brain cannot retain the information that it supposed to do especially when you are thinking of nothing but the comfort of your bed.

2. **Pay attention.** This may be the hardest thing to do – to pay attention. It takes a lot of concentrations and it is affected by inner and outside forces. There are also factors that would make us attend to the lectures and there are also some that would destroy our focus. Look at the teacher during the discussion. It is sometimes effective to imagine and form a visual structure of the information and everything that the teacher says. Focus your mind on the subject matter and do not be bothered with the noises around. Avoid looking at the ceiling or looking around the classroom as they hinder you from listening. More importantly, for you to pay attention, practice active listening. Do not just hear but understand the information.

3. **Take down notes.** This is a multi-tasking skill that every student must practice. It is essential to scribble down those important details that your professor says because there is a huge chance that it will come out in the test the day after. Note taking is not a verbatim writing. Instead, only those that are important and key points and expected. Now, there are those who take note according to their styles such as acronyms that are easier for them to understand, word short-cutting, initials, etc. Whatever it is that works for you, do it. Your notes serve

as the printed version of your teacher's memory so you better start taking down notes inside the class.

4. **Review the questions or notes.** Many students do not know the essentials of reviewing. It is one way to refresh your mind to the things that was discussed the previous day or the week prior. The printed materials you wrote count a lot in making your study time much easier and refreshing. Regular review of everything you have noted is a good practice to achieving the right result that you expect.

5. **Join study groups.** This is an optional activity among students. It depends on how comfortable you are in studying while being surrounded by number of people. However, this is also an effective way of learning. You can ask questions and even clarifications to the subject matter that seemed to be unclear to you. You can share ideas to one another hence, the fun and the camaraderie. As they always say, two heads are better than one.

6. **Put away devices.** Checking and sending emails, updating status on Facebook and twitter, texting, and constant using it are indeed multi-tasking activities but, not inside the classroom or whenever you want to maintain a good study environment. We are now surrounded with gadgets and any other technological devises that may destruct us from paying attention. Devices occupy your mind in thinking activities outside the class. *Phys Org* says that previous research has shown that students who text in class generally recall less about the classroom content than those who do not. Similarly, those who used mobile devices in class took notes of poorer quality, detracting from another cognitive process by which students integrate new

material. So, keeping away your mobiles and other gadgets during class and during review hours gives you the right amount of attention needed.

7. **Summarize your lessons.** This gives you an extra work, but this is a very effective way of retaining lessons you learned from school. Creating a summary of the entire chapter of the lesson is like giving yourself pointers and items of the things that will come out in the exams. This is also one way of reviewing because when you write, you also retain the information. This is effective among visual kind of learners because you'll tend to remember those words you wrote in the summary you created. And the funny thing is, you'll know which part of the paper you wrote it on. So, create a summary and do yourself a little bit of extra job that pays off.

8. **Choose your environment.** Your environment where you'll spend your time to study matters a lot in establishing the kind of learning you'll get. The cozier it is, the better. However; Let us take this as a subjective matter. There are people who could be able to concentrate well being surrounded by the noise, there are those who could be able to handle it well while listening to music, and there are those who could pull it off in a peaceful place. Know your style and keep it that way.

As it is important for college of high school students to study well to prepare for a better future. According to *Ashley Hill*, College is a hub of knowledge where most talented and professional lecturers give you the essence of their expertise and life experiences. For you to achieve your listed life-long goals, better start hitting the books with these effective suggestions as listed above.

6 Important Definitions of Excellent Customer Service

SERVICE WITH SINCERITY, WITH CLASS, AND WITH EXCELLENCE.

Coming up with a real definition of customer service made me do a profound thinking and contemplate if there's any. It is a vital aspect of business success in various industries specifically the *Business Process Outsource* or the BPO. In a sense of winning customer's loyalty, what really is a customer service? I made a list of its definition according to what I experienced and learned.

1. **It is giving your customer an honest answer on their questions.** Speaking with an irate customer for getting his enormous bill, is quite a difficult task. Customer will surely ask how on earth his bill became that high. As a representative of your company, all you could give to your customer is your consistent explanation and honesty to the reasons behind the increase. Now, there are some CSR or *customer service representative* who wouldn't give a damn explaining honestly to the customers just to get away with a long call that hurts their handling time.

2. **Customer Service means empathy.** Let us dig deeper as to why empathy makes a great customer service. As a human being, we are bombarded with several overwhelming emotions. We talk to hundreds of people each day who have different experiences and emotions. Some may have had a loved one passed away, some probably have just experienced heartbreaks, etc. Talking to a customer who is upset and hysterical with no apparent reason, yet the best thing we could offer

is sincere empathy with what they have been going through. Empathy with sincerity is different than just empathize for the sake of saying it. After all, it does not hurt to be nice and for customers, it is always hard to get mad at someone who is nice.

3. **Customer Service means resolving customer's issue in a timely manner.** Customers won't usually dwell for a long time over the phone talking to someone they don't know. They call or talk to you to get their problems resolved as fast as possible. Addressing their concerns quickly would make them happy and satisfied but of course without compromising the quality of your conversation. When you sound like you are in a hurry, the customer will know that you are not engaged, and you seem to be focused on ending the call.

4. **Customer Service means extending help to satisfy your customers.** I know that we are sometimes taught to resolve the very concern of the customers upon calling. However, customers will appreciate if help is extended especially if this is done in favor of them. Always remember that you are there to help them, make them happy and satisfied. Don't leave a room for a single frustration for some of their issues have not been resolved (though they sometimes forget to tell you first-hand a minor issue) because this will give them a bad customer experience. Asking them if there's anything else you could help them is a perfect phrase to extend help other than the resolved ones.

5. **Customer service means building rapport with the customers.** This may seem a little bit difficult for non-native English speakers. Asking how your day is, and how's the weather is overrated. Learning one's culture is

the key. As a representative, a soft skill must be perfected in order to connect with the customer. It is more than just asking usual questions that are often cracked by some of us, but it goes beyond that. Personalizing your call or calling them by their first name is one step towards connecting with your customers. Give a light tone, listen to their voice, listen to the background noise if there's any, and say something about it make it easier to build rapport with them. Be very cautious in inserting something funny when the customer is upset. You know what I am thinking right?

6. **Customer service means turning negative to positive.** You may be wondering how it becomes possible. "No", "I don't know", "I can't", "there's nothing more", etc. These are the words that a customer hates to hear. It is just about positive phrasing. This is part of the soft skills training that all of us must be aware of. If situation caught you off guard and you cannot do anything more, why don't you try the following sentences? *"I'm sorry but I cannot activate your service."* Instead, **"I can activate your service once the payment is made..."** or **"Here's what I can do..."**

"I don't know the answer to your questions." Instead, **"That is a good question, let me go ahead and find that out for you."**

Customer service is a very important skill that all of us must have in whatever kind of business we are in. This is the very soul of the business. The ability of one person to pacify an angry customer is a good example of showing a service that is world class. These tips do not only apply in a BPO industry, but all kinds of businesses that serve their customers. Always remember that an excellent customer service is equivalent to an excellent business.

How to be an Exceptional Telephone Conversationalist?

TELEPHONE ETIQUETTE

There are two sides of the story- the recipient and the caller himself. No matter which one you are, you have things to bear in mind in conversing on the phone. We are in a digital age and telephone is a vital equipment in communication in the office or in our normal lives. Below are the tips to consider:

<u>Receiving calls:</u>

1. **Answer the call with your normal voice and tone.** Your normal voice creates an identity that the person on the other line would know you easily and that also creates an impression. Speaking in a high-pitched tone may not be a good idea all the time in a certain speaking situation. A high volume and a high tone may be hurtful to the ears and that sounds an automatic phone drop.

2. **Answer clearly.** Clarity is one way to have a nice conversation on the phone as it reflects the effectiveness of the communication. You really don't want to speak with someone you can't understand a single word he is saying, do you? Speaking on the phone is a virtual face to face conversation and that requires clarity of what you are saying.

3. **Avoid eating or drinking.** This is important as this reflects the kind of person you are in dealing with your peers or customers over the phone. This is a professionalism that is beyond the attitude we should show to one another. This may also hinder the clarity and your focus in speaking with one another.

4. **Smile**. Take time to smile in answering the call as it resonates with your mood and the other person could see you smile. Yes, the other person could tell that you are smiling based on your tone. Smile for you will receive some good news!

5. **Focus**. The important factor to have an effective communication is "focus". Attend fully on the conversation itself as information may be as important as it might be for your career or for yourself. You don't want your colleague to repeat whatever he is saying because you don't get it the first or the second time. This is also an ingredient of an active listener.

Making calls:

1. **Introduce yourself properly**. Self-introduction is building rapport the person on the other line. Getting their attention to listen to you could make a pitch toward a successful conversation. When you are calling to someone you don't know personally, it is a good idea to tell him your name and the company you are working from and from then, you could tell your intention of calling. As a call receiver, I don't want to speak to someone who blurbs about a lot of things when in the first place I don't even know his name!

2. **Be polite**. There's no way a person could talk to someone who is rude unless you want the person hung up on your face!

3. **Avoid beating around the bush**. Be direct to the point as telephone conversation requires a short period of time. Nobody wants to speak long hours over the phone.

4. **Be the last one to hung up.** This is a polite way to end a conversation, for someone who initiates the call.

We are fortunate to live in a world where different media of communication are available for us. Let us consider using them to get its optimum purpose without compromising our professionalism and relationship with our peers. Make it a habit to deal with people with professionalism by observing these tips on telephone etiquette.

Simple Tips on How to Survive in College

College is perhaps one of the most difficult days in student's life. Living out of your comfort zone may be a bit of a challenge for some and it requires adjustment. Yes, it takes some time to adjust in an environment where people around you seem like strangers and do not care at all. There are different styles or techniques that students use in order to survive college. Here are some tips for your reference:

1. **Focus.** Pay attention to the reasons why you are in College. You are there to study and prepare for the challenges of life. Unfortunately, most of the students don't get why they are there in the first place. College is not an avenue of getting loose and getting drunk all night or any other forms of revenge in life. You are there to study and acquire a degree for a better life ahead.

2. **Choose your friend.** This is probably the most cliché phrase that you've read. But it is true. Your circle of friends has a big impact to your entire stay in college. They are your second family away from home. They influence the way you think and do today and tomorrow and it affects your behavior. As you can see, friends play

a major role in your life even in simple things like going out to a movie. I know that sometimes you don't want to go out alone and you wanted to bring your friends with you. Go to a restaurant, you have your friends with you. Go to the library, you have your friends with you. Go shopping, you have your friends with you, etc. It seems that we are surrounded by people every day no matter what we do, and we call them our friends.

3. **Know your professors.** Whether you like it or not, it is your professors who would make and break you. It is at the tip of their pen and on what kind of stroke they're going to use that would define your future at school. They may either pass you or fail you. So just a tip, know your professors. Know their way or methods of teaching for you to grasp the lessons easily. Moreover, kill their exams by learning the kind of test that they give and the items and keywords that they normally include. Remember, it is easy to study when you already have an idea of what will come out in the test.

4. **Get in touch with your loved ones.** There is no better cure of anxiety and nostalgia than seeing and keeping your family and loved ones at your side. College life is different. Sometimes you need to live by yourself away from them. That's part of the process of learning to be independent. To avoid nostalgia, be in touched with your friends and family. The innovation of technology is right in front of us. We can now send them emails, send SMS, make calls, internet aided communications such as video messaging and stuff like that. It is now easier to communicate in today's world and so this helps.

5. **Have fun.** Don't forget that we are a social being. We need to define our purpose and at the same time

have fun in dealing with life. College is not all about studying; but studying while having fun is a different story and integration is the key. Go out with your friends if time permits. Socialize in a moderate way but do not compromise your schedule of classes and examination days. More importantly, bear in mind not to over-do it and know your limits. This is one way of finding motivations to do more and be resilient in everything we do. Once we find fulfillment and fun, it is easier to cope with challenges that we face every day.

These tips may be of great help for some - not considering the monetary reasons though. Whether you are in college or planning to go to college, this is the time for you to examine yourself and take a big decision of your life. As I said, college is not easy, and it takes a lot of effort and smart approach to survive. Remember, struggle may be real, but the fruit after college and employment is the sweetest.

These are 5 Things that make you a Professional

THINGS PEOPLE LOOK AND IDENTIFY PROFESSIONALS

No matter how good you are, people will have something to say about you. Being good does not always warrant people's respect but how you make them feel will have an impact and give an impression that will make them like you. In other words, professionalism is something intangible that people notice about you. How does one establish professionalism in the workplace or in all situations? Below are the tips that make you professional:

1. **The way you communicate.** Communication is a powerful tool that connects you to one another. It is one

way to establish an identity that will make people like you. The way one communicates should anchor with respect whether it is written or verbal communication. How you deal with people in the office will be your manner of communicating. It will either make or break your impression to them as a professional. A truthful communication and a friendly approach are a sign of credibility that you establish yourself for.

2. **Punctuality.** If you are someone who respects people, you are someone who respect their time as well by being on time or even ahead of time during meetings. You are someone who adheres to the time set in the office and you religiously follow the rules. This is a sign of professionalism that cannot be taught on someone because this kind of responsibility is something that must come from within.

3. **The way you look.** Talking about how we should look as a person speaks a lot about us being professional. Wearing appropriate dress in the office does not necessarily mean wearing fancy or expensive clothes. One should look neat and tidy because that is a sign that you can handle yourself well - talking about time management. Appropriate clothing in the office is encouraged because you are surrounded by professionals in different fields. The way you look is an emblem that you are one of them, you are one of those who take pride about your profession.

4. **The way you treat your colleagues.** No matter how many degrees you earn or how high your title is, does not guarantee you as a true professional. Your treatment to your colleagues does! Being good to people and not looking down at them is a characteristic of a professional individual. You are not someone who

degrades or belittles others because of their low position in the company. You should be the one to encourage and influence them to strive hard and earn a higher position. Arrogance is never congruent to professionalism.

5. **Adherence to the rules.** People who follow even just a simple rule is a sign of professionalism. This is probably one of the most difficult tasks for others to do – to follow the rules. Be the one who sticks to the rules even if it means that you should sacrifice your habit that you used to have that should not be brought to the office. Be the one who is happy enough to lead in following the rules, and not breaking them.

The life of a career individual is bound with several rules and provisions – it might be in the office or a norm set by the society. However, we should know that being professional should something that you feel good about and make you a successful person or a leader. Professionalism is not only limited to the above 5 elements, but it is more than that. We should discover more and learn from those influential and successful people in the business. Added to that, be mindful with the way you act around people and be sensitive towards their feelings. Let us remind ourselves with the famous rule, *"Do unto others what you want others do unto you."*

Tips for Writing a Stirring Graduation Speech

A TOP OF THE CLASS SPEECH THAT MAGNIFIES THE HEARTS OF LISTENERS.

Graduation day is a momentous for graduating students. There are students who are gifted with intelligence and made them on top of their class and as a result, a privilege to speak and deliver inspiring remarks to his fellow graduates. If you are one of those "gifted" and smart graduates, this article is for you as a guide in writing your graduation speech that lasts a lifetime.

1. **Begin with acknowledgment and gratitude.** Okay, this is basic, but basic is important. Let us show them that being smart is a total package with the right amount of attitude and enough skills. Acknowledge the people around you especially the guests who spent their time to be with you in your graduation day despite their hectic schedules. Thank your parents who are very proud watching you and listening to every word you say. Mind you, they are the proudest people on earth. Your teachers deserve it too! They untiringly and willingly spent almost of the time of their life buckling down for you!

2. **Talk about your experience that inspires.** Every person experienced ups and downs. It would be great if you could share your experience that draws lessons, inspirations, and which made you strive harder. This is the time to let people see that setbacks are not a bad thing at all.

3. **Integrate humor.** I think you already have an idea why. The attention span of people listening to your speech may not be as lengthy as your speech itself so giving them a humorous statement from time to time would make a huge difference. This is one way of keeping your listeners engaged and focused on you.

4. **State a quote that inspires.** The quotations that you include in your speech must be the ones coming from famous or "well-known" individuals with whom people easily identify. They are those who exist to inspire and teach lessons of a lifetime. Such quotations will make

an impact on your speech as they are the reflection of the truth of life.

5. **Write whenever you feel relaxed.** This is an important consideration in writing a speech. A state of relaxed mind and body is a great time to write an inspirational speech. The train of thought will flow smoothly according to what you think and feel. This is also the time when you feel at your best and will make you motivated.

6. **Mean every word you write and say.** Be truthful not because you are on top but because you want to leave an impact to them. A good speech is coming from the heart, not for the sake of creating a brilliant one with no heart in it.

7. **End with a bang.** An open-ended question perhaps will work. I don't know. It's up to you on how to end your speech that will make quite an impact. A cheer maybe or the one hell of a humorous statement. Well, relevant joke of the century will do, or the like as the last scene before the commercial break. You decide.

We all want to be on top of our game, and a graduation moment feels like it. Writing to influence and inspire people is not easy. It takes a lot of effort, thinking, and heart are needed to make this happen. It is my honor to share with you these tips on how to write a stirring graduation speech that lasts a lifetime.

*** END***

REFERENCES

McLeod L., (September 2019). Hire, Retain, and Grow Top Millennial Talent. Retrieved from https://www.linkedin.com/learning/how-to-hire-retain-and-grow-top-millennial-talent/treat-your-employees-like-a-number-and-they-ll-return-the-favor

Neill C., (April 2016). Forbes. 12 Tips for Public Speaking. Retrieved from: https://www.forbes.com/sites/iese/2016/04/18/12-tips-for-public-speaking/#4c1637893a18

Peerver J. and Murray B., (September 2015). What happens in the brain during sleep?. Retrieved from https://www.scientificamerican.com/article/what-happens-in-the-brain-during-sleep1/

Taylor F., (June 2015). Phys Org. How do Mobile Devices in the classroom impact student learning? Retrieved from https://phys.org/news/2015-06-mobile-devices-classroom-impact-student.html

Gillett R., (May 2017). Business Insider. 38 things you should remove from your resume before it ends up in the 'no' pile. Retrieved from https://www.businessinsider.com/things-to-remove-from-resume-2017-5

Green A., (June 2017). US News. Five Interview Lines That Make Job Interviewers Cringe. Retrieved from https://money.usnews.com/money/blogs/outside-voices-careers/articles/2017-06-12/5-interview-lines-that-make-job-interviewers-cringe

Watson K., (November 2016). Healthline. The Top 7 Mental Benefits of Sports. Retrieved from https://www.healthline.com/health/mental-benefits-sports

Emamzadeh A., (September 2018). Psychology Today. Workplace Bullying: Causes, Effects, and Preventions. Retrieved from https://www.psychologytoday.com/us/blog/finding-new-home/201809/workplace-bullying-causes-effects-and-prevention

Riordan C., (July 2013). Business Harvard Review. We all need friends at work. Retrieved from https://hbr.org/2013/07/we-all-need-friends-at-work

Gallo C., (April 2017). Forbes. College Seniors: 65% of recruiters say this one skill is more important than your major. Retrieved from https://www.forbes.com/sites/carminegallo/2017/04/30/college-seniors-65-percent-of-recruiters-say-this-one-skill-is-more-important-than-your-major/#369bbd0d757c

Taylor J., (May 2011). Huffpost. Confidence matters for athletes. Retrieved from https://www.huffingtonpost.com/dr-jim-taylor/confidence-matters-for-at_b_827666.html

Barber T., (March 2012). Men's Health. Wear the Right Watch at an Interview. Retrieved from www.menshealth.co.uk/style/watches/wear-the-right-watch-at-an-interview

Viscusi S., (September 2013). Huffpost. Watch Yuorself Get a Job: Why I believe a wristwatch can land you a job. Retrieved from https://www.huffingtonpost.com/stephen-viscusi/watch-yourself-get-a-job-_b_3654560.html

Bradberry T., (February 2017). TalentSmart. Multitasking damages your brain and your career, new study suggests. Retrieved from http://www.talentsmart.com/articles/Multitasking-Damages-Your-Brain-and-Your-Career%2C-New-Studies-Suggest-2102500909-p-1.html

Huhman H., (July 2018). Glassdoor. 5 phrases to close your cover letter and land the interview. Retrieved from https://www.glassdoor.com/blog/5-phrases-close-cover-letter-land-interview/

Verlinden N., (March 2018). Human Resources Today. The power of an employee referral program. Retrieved from http://www.humanresourcestoday.com/?query=Referrals&open-article-id=7963889&article-title=the-power-of-an-employee-referral-program&blog-domain=digitalhrtech.com&blog-title=digital-hr-tech

Mckay D.R., (November 2018). The Balance Careers. How to set short and long term goals for your career. Retrieved from https://www.thebalancecareers.com/goal-setting-526182

Carlson A., (October 2012). Drinking Stress Away: The Link Between Water and Stress Reduction. Retrieved from http://www.stresspandemic.com/blog/drinking-stress-away-the-link-between-water-and-stress-reduction

Other Online References:

Bullying law and Legal Definition. Retrieved from https://definitions.uslegal.com/b/bullying/

Staff Human Resources, Examples of Bullying behaviors. Retrieved from https://shr.ucsc.edu/elr/abusive-conduct-and-bullying-in-the-workplace/examples-of-bullying-behavior.html

The role of a reward in employee motivation. Retrieved from https://smallbusiness.chron.com/role-reward-employee-motivation-18814.html

The hard conversation you need to prep for if your job's on the line. Retrieved from https://www.themuse.com/advice/the-hard-conversation-you-need-to-prep-for-if-your-jobs-on-the-line

Top ten reasons why you need a cover letter. Retrieved from https://www.monstergulf.com/career-advice/top-ten-reasons-why-you-need-a-cover-letter-230.html

Interview Tips that Lead to Job Offers. Retrieved from http://www.monster.co.uk/career-advice/article/top-5-job-interview-tips

Interview tips: 10 tips to improve interview performance. Retrieved from https://www.monster.com/career-advice/article/boost-your-interview-iq

10 Best Job Interview Tips for Jobseekers. Retrieved from https://www.livecareer.com/career/advice/interview/job-interview-tips

Social Media Recruiting. Retrieved from https://hiring.monster.com/hr/hr-best-practices/recruiting-hiring-advice/attracting-job-candidates/recruiting-via-social-media.aspx

www.ingramcontent.com/pod-product-compliance
Lightning Source LLC
Chambersburg PA
CBHW030812180526
45163CB00003B/1242